Roslyn Schwartz is a psychotherapist specializing in marital problems. She is also Secretary of the American Academy of Psychotherapists.

Leonard Schwartz is a practicing clinical psychologist in Brightwaters, New York. He is on the faculties of Heed and Adelphi Universities and is currently working on new therapy techniques for couples and families.

Becoming a Couple

MAKING THE MOST OF EVERY STAGE OF YOUR RELATIONSHIP

ROSLYN SCHWARTZ
LEONARD J. SCHWARTZ

A SPECTRUM BOOK

PRENTICE-HALL, INC. Englewood Cliffs, New Jersey 07632

Library of Congress Cataloging in Publication Data

SCHWARTZ, ROSLYN.
  Becoming a couple.

  (A Spectrum book)
  Includes index.
    1. Marriage.   2. Love.   3. Interpersonal
relations.   4. Self-actualization (Psychology)
I. Schwartz, Leonard J., joint author.   II. Title.
HQ734.S416   306.8   80-11960
ISBN   0-13-072173-5
ISBN   0-13-072165-4 (pbk.)

Editorial/production supervision and interior design by Suse L. Cioffi
Cover design by Michael Aron
Manufacturing buyer: Cathie Lenard

PRENTICE-HALL INTERNATIONAL, INC., *London*
PRENTICE-HALL OF AUSTRALIA PTY. LIMITED, *Sydney*
PRENTICE-HALL OF CANADA, LTD., *Toronto*
PRENTICE-HALL OF INDIA PRIVATE LIMITED, *New Delhi*
PRENTICE-HALL OF JAPAN, INC., *Tokyo*
PRENTICE-HALL OF SOUTHEAST ASIA PTE. LTD., *Singapore*
WHITEHALL BOOKS LIMITED, *Wellington, New Zealand*

Dedication

This book is dedicated to the memory of Kenneth A. Fisher, Ira Parnes, and Samuel Schwartz. They were great teachers through the expression of their individuality in marriage. This book is also dedicated to the aliveness of the women they married: Kathleen Dunning, Shirley Klavan, and Lillian Snow.

CONTENTS

ACKNOWLEDGMENTS

We gratefully acknowledge the importance of Sonia and Morton Goldstein and Lynn and Mickey Gross in helping us understand and accept our coupling process and generating many of the ideas presented in this book. We also wish to acknowledge the importance of our parents, Shirley and Ira Parnes and Lillian and Samuel Schwartz. They modeled loyalty and devotion to family and a commitment to marriage despite many obstacles. Our own struggle to recognize our expectations while remaining connected to the real people in our lives has been forcefully abetted by our children: Ellen, Debra, Judith, and Karen.

For inspiration and encouragement we are particularly grateful to Carol and Gerald C. Davison. Don and Millie Broughton deserve credit for gently but persuasively goading us into writing down our ideas. John Warkentin and Elizabeth Valerius read and commented on the early part of the book. Their suggestions helped propel the rest of the manuscript. Joan Fagan, Irma Shepherd, Vivian Guze, Gladys Natchez, David Hawkins, and Felice Gans all read parts of the book, making valuable contributions toward firming up the theory of couple formation and development.

We are thankful to Stuart Valins and Judith Waldman for their suggestions and advice regarding basic research in the theory. Melvin D. Schwartz and Jerrold M. Becker helped in making parts of the manuscript more readable. To Debra and Jerry Kramer go our deep gratitude for helping to provide the energy and encouragement in overcoming our resistance to The Honeymoon Is Over and Giving Up.

While we were preparing the book, Pat Sadler was most gracious in her availability to type the manuscript many times. David Sterling and Judith Frankel were invaluable in reproducing the text at various stages in its development. We are particularly thankful to Lynne Lumsden, whose support and encouragement remained consistent from the beginning.

Finally, to our many patients and students who openly shared their lives and struggles with us goes our heartfelt appreciation. Working out the details of their relationships over the years provided the raw material from which this book grew.

INTRODUCTION

During the past thirty years a veritable revolution has taken place in the institution of marriage. Since World War II we have witnessed the widespread use of contraception, the women's liberation movement, technological changes that have led to an increased alienation between people, and news media that have quickened the pace of information transmittal. These and other factors have combined to make the traditional marriage an anachronism. We have seen communal living, co-ed dormitories, sexual liberation, gay activists, and innumerable alternative styles of coupling. Obviously, the old ways that men and women joined to form a family can no longer be taken for granted. The search for more gratifying and fulfilling interaction between the sexes has challenged many of our preconceived ideas of what makes a happy union. We seem to have a better perspective on what is wrong with conventional marriages but few answers as to how to improve this institution.

During the past three decades many efforts at increasing happiness involved changing the stylized roles of husband and wife. The 1950s emphasized the needless drudgery of housework and the liberation of women by countless household appliances. The Pill was introduced, enabling family planning. Both men and women sought greater freedom from the routine tasks of family management. With increased material security came the search for self-fulfillment and personal expansiveness. The 1960s saw consciousness raising and an assault on sexual inequality. Gender roles were uprooted. Men as well as women began to question their attitudes toward the sexes. The tranquility of once-set roles in marriage turned to confusion and disorder. Dissatisfactions were abundant; solutions were not readily forthcoming. The 1970s opened with a questioning of much of our values as a people and a readiness to discard systems no longer functionally useful. The divorce rate skyrocketed. The birth rate fell below zero population growth. One after another, traditions that previously seemed inviolate gave way to changing values. Marriage and the family as the basic stable unit of society was most threatened by this churning discontent.

Increasingly, couples sought relief from their unhappiness by turning to psychologists. The professionals were ill prepared to meet this challenge. During the first half of the century, psychotherapy focused almost entirely on the individual. Nowhere was there a comprehensive grasp of couple formation and marital development. Under pressure to relieve the symptoms of marital dysfunction, psychologists began to offer limited solutions. Masters and Johnson innovated sex therapy. Jackson and his associates shed new light on communication problems within the family. The behavior modification practitioners provided faster means to achieve desirable behaviors. Many serious and dedicated clinicians studied and confronted the troubled marriage with a variety of therapeutic interventions. Although these systems helped alleviate some of the difficulties in marriage, they failed to provide a guideline for a working grasp of marital development.

We have evolved, from our twenty-five years of experience in treating couples, a concept of pair formation and marital development. This formulation has as its base the belief that people reach maturity and form relationships founded on their early parent-child experiences. We learn about attachment, caring, and intimacy—the main ingredients in a love relationship—from the manner and quality of love we received as children. The closeness we had with our nurturing parent, whether mother, father, grandmother, or other significant person, set the stage for our expectations and behavior in intimate relationships. This early symbiotic love, being the first, was the most impressionable experience in connecting to another. The fulfillment and gratification obtained became the standard by which we measured all subsequent interactions. Out of this union our self-image emerged. The idealized picture of our lover is based on this experience. Early learned scripts govern the patterns of our later family formation. We leave the nest programmed to recapitulate our most significant tie to another.

In addition to the formation of a coupling similar to our early symbiotic tie, we tend to evolve in this relationship through developmental stages that parallel the phases of parent–child interaction. Beginning with the symbiosis we gradually individuate through discrete but overlapping steps until we establish a stable equalitarian relationship. Inherent in the symbiotic and romantic love unions is the paradox of remaining dependently connected to a person to whom we attribute magical benevolent powers while we develop the confidence and the skills to independently satisfy ourselves. The fantasies and expectations projected onto our significant other can only be fulfilled if we remain in an infantile state. Our growth and development necessitate a modification and more realistic view of both ourselves and our mate. The manner in which we modify our behavior generally follows a sequential progression patterned after our experiences in the parent–child relationship.

The romantic coupling, consisting of a melding of two separate, unique individuals, each with their own fantasy of a loving other, cannot possibly be sustained. As our natural growth altered and challenged the symbiosis with our mother, so too does the emergence of adult needs modify and upset the balance in marriage. The increase in our self-sufficiency requires a realignment of the coupling. This change necessitates the recognition and acceptance of the respective individualities of each member of the union. The process of individuation in one partner challenges the fantasy of the other. Each spouse assumes that the loving connection is experienced reciprocally. This assumption of the nature of love leads to expectations that cannot be realized. The ensuing disappointment is most often felt as a rejection and separation from our beloved.

To remain positively joined the couple must accommodate to the reality of their changing individualities while maintaining their caring and intimate posture. As in childhood, the greatest fear of the unilateral pursuit of our own needs is that we will be rejected and abandoned. We tend to respond to this fear in a manner similar to that of our youth. The reaction of our mate to this anxiety sets up a dynamic interplay between both partners. This interaction gives rise to an unfolding pattern and sequence of marital stages designed to accommodate the contradictions inherent in coupling. The pattern develops in ways that closely parallel the formative stages of the growing youngster in the parent–child interaction. The parent–child relationship also has to deal effectively with the issues of loving connections and individual needs. How a youngster manages to remain joined to his or her parent while evolving a separate personhood lays the groundwork for the subsequent pattern of adjustment to a mate. While there tends to be discrete sequential steps in this pattern, the overlapping and length of time in any one phase is a function of the early developmental experience. Some couples remain in the romantic phase of marriage for years. Others begin to individuate right after the honeymoon. Most newlyweds retain their illusions of love even while grappling with the realities of their mate. Some renounce their fantasies in order to deal more effectively with each other's true personality. There are as many combinations and variations of marriage as there are parent–child relationships. Some are more passionate and joyous than others. Some are more secure and predictable. Regardless of specific styles of interaction, all couples must learn to cope with the inevitable disillusionment of their expectations and to replace such wishes with a growing appreciation and respect for their partner. If this is not accomplished the marriage will be painful and may dissolve. Success in this endeavor can lead to a genuine respect for each other and an equalitarian relationship that is fulfilling to both.

Understanding the marital process can help couples overcome the discomfort and helplessness frequently experienced in dealing with the pitfalls of marriage. Recognizing the various stages of marital development and identifying where one stands in this process can eliminate the confusion and hopelessness of some pairs. Perceiving how the relationship may evolve provides a perspective to bring about the needed adjustments to the dyad. Most important of all, viewing marriage as a developmental process offers a no-fault structure within which partners can perceive each other more clearly. If husbands and wives could only substitute blaming each other for their unhappiness with a sense of the complexity and contradiction inherent in their involvement, perhaps they could again begin talking with excited interest in each other. It is our hope that this book will be of some help to that end.

1
chapter

THE LOVING
RELATIONSHIP

Being in love is like magic. You feel great, you like yourself, you are happy in the present and euphoric about the future. Everywhere you look colors are brighter, sounds are sharper, tastes are keener, smells are more fragrant, and touches are exquisite. People seem happier; they certainly respond to you with greater joy and élan. Even though you are sometimes distracted in your work thinking of your loved one, when you do apply yourself, you are totally involved and generally more efficient. You are more innovative, more "open" and expressive, and frequently more creative. You are in better health than usual and feel firmer, smoother, and sprier. You love yourself feeling this way.

When you are with your beloved, life is complete. You have everything you want for the moment. You see the beauty in your loved one and have no doubt that it will be there forever. The one you love smells sweet, has a glow that lights up the room. You feel secure, trusting, "at home" with this person. You are more self-revealing in this relationship than in any other. You want to open up and present yourself totally to your lover. You can't get too close. You want to fuse, become

1

one. You can't be together enough. Even when you have un-imaginably pleasurable sex, it is not enough. You want to be inside your lover. You want your lover to be inside you. All stoppers are gone. You flow toward the one you cherish and, in turn, feel the easy current of your dear one in and around you. There is no question that you belong to each other, for you two are special: you are truly in love.

Parting from your lover is painful. You feel torn. You feel as though a section of your body is missing. When separated, you think about this "part" of yourself most of the time. You replay vignettes of yesterday, last night, a week ago, when you were together. These mental pictures warm and nourish you. They bring a smile to your face. You can't wait to be rejoined. You telephone, drop by for lunch, incorporate going on an errand with being together. You find excuses to be close. This total absorption with your loved one is accompanied by a loss of weight and a gradual withdrawal from all activities and people except for the one you desire. The wish and need to be united becomes so all-encompassing you decide to live to-gether, to get married, to share the same space all the time. It is too painful to suffer the separation from your "other half."

Thus, couples are formed. The social, familial, economic, and legal forces surrounding this dyad further solidify the union. The world can't help but become infected by the bliss, the warmth, the positive energy flowing from this pair. Almost everyone wants to feel and look like they do. They are winners. They have what we all seek—love.

At times, the pair act strangely. They communicate in baby talk, through a glance or a touch. They seem like children in their naive openness. They are so trusting of each other and, to a greater extent than usual, of the world around them, that they appear vulnerable. They are having fun. They look as if they are perpetually at play. They whisper and giggle like ado-lescents. They laugh heartily, as though on cue, at a seemingly commonplace event. Yet they are serious in attending to each other's needs. They act as though to please their mate is to please themselves. They feel needed, wanted, and important in fulfilling each other. Their sense of responsibility in bringing comfort and joy to their partner leaves no doubt they are determined adults unconditionally concerned for each other as deeply as are mothers for their newborn.

BEHAVIORAL ROOTS

In fact, the tenderness displayed by a couple in love has as its closest prototype the loving care that a mother gives her young child. The devotion, attentiveness, and unconditional nature of a mother's love is rarely experienced by the child again until he or she grows to maturity and falls in love. Significantly, to most children who have been lovingly cared for and gently weaned, love comes relatively easily as they enter adolescence and beyond. Those youngsters whose needs were not adequately met, or who were precipitously told to "stop being a baby," enter maturity with enough self-doubt and mistrust of finding a partner who will sustain a loving attitude toward them that they find it difficult to love or be loved. However, everyone who has reached maturity and functions within the limits of normality has been loved. This state of early concern and fulfillment is imprinted on us all. Somewhere, we "remember" how it felt to have another human being take care of us. We take this memory with us as we mature. Ultimately, it becomes our model, our expectation of a loving relationship.

In combination with our sense of being mothered, we develop into adulthood with a personality and character structure that is predicated on our being a "good child." That is, we evolve, usually through trial and error, a habitual, stylized behavioral pattern that is fostered, supported, and approved by the significant adults in our environment. Children are naturally spontaneous and authentically self-expressive. They are also dependent on their parents. This dependency includes proper physical as well as emotional care. The affective aspect of this solicitude includes touching, stroking, and holding, as well as speaking warmly and approvingly to the young child. A baby develops a sense of value, worth, and importance through the quality of physical and emotional attention he or she receives. As the youngster develops, he or she learns which behavior elicits parental approval and which elicits censure. The child's confident self-image emerges as he or she acquires those skills that increase the positive and decrease the negative feedback received from those upon whom he or she is dependent. This feedback eventually leads to the youngster's renunciation of spontaneity for circumscribed behavior that fits the family's value system.

This circumscribed behavior includes the child's ability to protect the mother's self-image of one who fulfills her offspring's needs even when it is not true. Children can often be seen agreeing that they are happy, are not afraid of the dark, or like to eat spinach in order to placate an anxious parent. The self-deprecating and dishonest reponse to avoid hurting a parent is part of the learned skill required later to avoid discord in adult relationships. Couples are constantly reassuring each other that they are content and fulfilled even when they are not. It is not uncommon to hear of a wife who has faked orgasms so that her husband would not question his masculinity. Similarly, a husband often speaks in glowing terms of his wife's cooking while barely touching his food.

During the early years of life, a child's skill in making parents feel effective and accomplished in caring for him or her generally evokes approval. The child learns how to receive care. As he or she develops, the child will trade off pursuing personal wishes for parental approval. Through repetition and redundancy, this behavior evolves into an organized set of responses and actions. The personality and character ultimately fashioned from this training thus includes the youngster's knowledge of how to be a good child. Accordingly, the youngster grows up with a sense of the kind of mothering he or she has had, and wants again, along with an awareness of how he or she must behave in order to obtain love.

SYMBIOSIS

The early mother–child relationship is a symbiotic one. That is, the needs and gratifications of each are respectively fulfilled by the other. In utero, the fetus requires nourishment and an outlet for its wastes through the mother's bloodstream. The mother, in turn, needs a healthy fetus to absorb her nutrients and develop into a normal baby in order for her body to fulfill its procreative function. After birth, the baby needs milk to survive. The mother needs the discomfort of her full breasts relieved by having them pleasantly sucked. The baby needs to be fed solid food. The mother opens her mouth as she places the spoon on the child's lips. The mother needs to feel needed and effective in fulfilling the child. The child is dependent on the mother and is satisfied when fulfilled. The two are mutually dependent. They need each other and they satisfy each other.

Similarly, adult loving relationships are symbiotic in nature. Each partner has needs and gratifications associated with the other. Each must feel needed and effective in fulfilling his or her mate in order to sustain the loving connection. This requires that each spouse be both a good mother *and* a good child. Each must be sensitive and caring of the other and each must also be capable of being fulfilled by the other. Thus, a mature, responsible behavior pattern must be accompanied by an *ability to regress,* to be a "good child." Much of the childlike behavior we see in lovers stems from this regressive requirement of the symbiosis. Through this acting out of early patterns of conduct, each partner learns what pleases his or her mate and is in a better position to offer gratification. In our culture, it is often difficult for men to permit themselves to regress, as they tend to view their dependency as unmanly. However, in a loving relationship this is usually overcome in the exclusivity of the coupling.

This exclusivity also has its roots in the child-rearing process. Despite the presence of another parent, siblings, and other relatives, the infant views the mothering environment as existing solely for its benefit. Coming from the mother's womb, the newborn cannot discern where self ends and the supportive surroundings begin. Everything and everyone in this universe is here for its comfort and existence. Whether the mothering one is the natural mother, father, grandparent, older sibling, or friend, the infant makes no distinction between "me" and "not me." Not until the baby is aware that it is hungry, wet, or cold and experiences discomfort, does the earliest sense of a "not me" enter anything like a consciousness. At this point in its development, the baby, mostly through a series of random behavioral patterns, learns to manipulate the concerned environment in order to eliminate its discomfort. Crying, rocking, banging on the side of the crib, throwing down a rattle, all become part of the repertoire of the young child to satisfy its needs. Smiling, cooing, sucking, swallowing, and belching on cue for a significant adult further add to its power to attract and sustain a loving, dependent connection to a parent. The young child displays no concern for, nor awareness of, the mothering one's connection to others. As far as the baby is concerned, this parent is on call twenty-four hours a day, seven days a week, solely to meet its needs as they arise. There is no awareness that the mothering one has any needs other than those related to the baby. He or she belongs to the baby-to the exclusion of all.

Loving couples also display this sense of exclusivity. No other person, no other interest, no force is greater than the power of this unity. Not only are both partners attentive to each other, they are not individually attentive to anyone or anything else. If they should take time out from being alone to befriend another, they do so as a couple. Both in concert, as a dyad, experience a new individual, an event, a meal, or a sunset. When you are in love, what good is a beautiful sunset without a loving partner? Whatever is "not them" they share and incorporate into their marriage. Their repertoire and ability to enjoy their surroundings will depend on their collective skills and experience in successfully interacting with their milieu in a fashion that does not threaten their exlusivity. The sunset must never become more important than the spouse's ability to enjoy it.

THE BIG FEAR

Inherent in this need for exclusivity is the Big Fear. The big fear of every lover is that someday this loved one will leave. Being left all alone is a universal worry that everyone must encounter. For most of us this concept is equivalent to, or worse than, facing death—the ultimate state of aloneness. It is most poignant when we have formed a symbiotic attachment to another. The loss of this significant individual is often experienced as a loss of the best part of oneself. No wonder deep depression, withdrawal, or even suicide frequently accompanies the death of a loved one.

We are so sensitive to this loss, and the associated fear, that the slightest hint of a separation causes us to worry. Criticism, rejection, unavailability, or our mate's intimate involvement with another person, is enough to make us feel insecure. Finding that our mate is having an affair is enough to panic most of us. During the early stages of a loving relationship, such feelings of fear are generally accompanied by confusion, hurt, guilt, and an increased attempt to please our spouse. Because we are symbiotically connected, we believe that making our mate happy will relieve our pain. Thus, in order to overcome our own discomfort, we try to please our partner.

The equivalent of such a relationship can be seen between parent and child. A youngster lost on a beach or in a crowd generates anxiety in both parent and offspring. Scolding a child will often give rise to the youngster's crying painfully as though being abandoned. Frequently, punishment is meted out by sending a youngster to his or her room to be alone. In turn, a child can often get what he or she wants by hiding or acting hurt or angry. Telling mother she is unloving or isn't the "real" mother is often enough to cause the parent to offer all kinds of reassuring proof that such charges are untrue. Thus, children learn to "be good" to avoid losing a parent and the parent's love. They also develop skills to manipulate others to obtain the approval they seek. At maturation, such talents are incorporated into the individual's personality and serve as the basis for effective dealings with others. In a loving relationship, the use of such traits is heightened as the intensity of fear of losing the loved one increases.

THE LOVE FANTASY

People in love seem invincible. Their optimism is unlimited. They convey an air of complete confidence. No obstacle is too great to overcome in order to sustain their love. Neither social nor familial disapproval, religious nor ethnic differences, financial limitations, conditions of health, nor any other hindrance can stand in the way of two lovers forming a unity. They can do anything. They are grandiose in their appraisal of their skills and capacity to make this union a success. Love conquers all.

This, too, has its origins in the parent–child relationship. As the infant gradually learns to interact successfully with its environment to minimize discomforts and to increase satisfactions, its sense of power heightens. By the fourth year of life, a child's sense of mastery over those in his or her surroundings peaks. The child demands his or her own way and refuses to comply with any restrictions or limitations that would curtail fulfillment of his or her goals. The child appears omnipotent, pitting self against the significant adults in order to get his or her own way. The "fearsome fours" are a time to try any parent's patience. It is also a period when the youngster learns to test the limits of his or her power.

One symbol of the child's ultimate power is the ability to "possess" the loved parent. Attempts to have an exclusive relationship with the loved adult on the child's own terms reach a climax at this time. Eventually, out of fear of punishment and abandonment and a sense of guilt in hurting the loved parent, the youngster renounces this stand of grandiosity and faces reality.

OEDIPAL RESOLUTION

By age seven, most children have given up trying to get their own way and have learned to comply with the standards and value systems of their parents. They are able to learn from their culture and can leave home long enough to develop the necessary skills for successful living by attending school. However, this renunciation of power, this giving up of the loved parent as an exclusive possession, is predicated on the belief (reinforced by parents and society) that if he or she is a "good" child, identifies with the parent of the same sex, and learns the skills necessary for success, the youngster can have the "reward" when he or she matures. This prize is the exclusive possession of a loved one in a mutually satisfying and fulfilling relationship. Thus, the Oedipus stage is resolved by temporarily holding in abeyance the reward for good behavior. We enter adulthood after ten or more years of deprivation and subjection of our will to that of society with a promise that nirvana is at the end of this path. It is not surprising, then, that the attainment of a loving relationship is so heavily charged with emotion and energy. That is where everything comes together. All those years of trying, learning, waiting, and dreaming of the time when we can grow up, and really obtain what we want to be happy, fall into place when we fall in love. It is fantastic when it happens.

When you consider that two people, raised separately, with different loving parents, having spent years holding in check their respective yearnings for an exclusive love affair, come together with expectations and dreams of what this relationship will be like, it is magical that they can make it happen. Certainly, it helps to form such a union if each member initially believes that his or her mate possesses all the qualities associated with the loving parent. This belief further helps foster and bring out those loving traits of which each partner is potentially capable. However, as both young people are projecting onto each other their concepts of a loving partner, they must eventually reconcile their fantasies with reality. The greater the discrepancy between the projected expectations and the actual personality and character of the spouse, the more difficult it will become to face the reality of this relationship. People with strong fantasies and high expectations are more likely to be disappointed with their mates after the honeymoon than those who are less so inclined. All lovers, however, must learn to accept and get along with the real person rather than continue their projections onto this individual.

Traditionally, most couples go on a honeymoon immediately after the wedding. This experience is important and often sets the stage for the ensuing style of marriage. On this vacation the two individuals are free to explore each other without the pressures or concerns of work, family, or society. Since neither partner has taken a course in marital practices and behavior, their interaction is based on their respective experiences and fantasies in family organization and operation. A great deal of their expectations also comes from the idealized image of marriage presented in the movies and on television. There is generally a heightened excitement in being together, leading to frequent and intense sex. The pleasure and joy of being fulfilled and effective in gratifying each other confirm their judgment that they, indeed, are special. The closer the actual experience is to expectation, the more confident and assured the couple are in their decision to marry. Invariably, however, in some dimensions of their interaction reality does not measure up to fantasy. Most couples are so eager to please and be pleased that they ignore this disappointment. That is, while the unfulfilled wish is registered in consciousness, it is not usually discussed and dealt with openly. Both are too busy enjoying the bliss of the union. As long as they are free of other responsibilities, they can devote themselves to delighting each other. In time, the honeymoon must come to an end and the newly married pair must return to the daily responsibilities of work, money, housekeeping, and visiting relatives. Now the focus of the marriage must shift. The couple must learn to deal with the realities of living as a unit without the benefit of constant positive reinforcement from each other. The working through of the marital arrangement begins.

2
chapter

THE HONEYMOON IS OVER

Returning from their honeymoon, Julie and Tom joyously set out to find an apartment of their own. Holding hands and smiling, they enter the first two room walk-up on their list. After a quick glance at the bathroom and hall closet Tom announces, "We'll take it." Julie says that she would like to look at some of the others on their schedule. She thinks the apartment is too small and drab. Tom points out that the rooms seem intimate and the dark green walls feel romantic to him. Julie becomes increasingly upset with the thought that her husband is more attached to this apartment than to her. He seems relatively unconcerned about her feelings. Julie begins to feel uncertain. She has assumed that Tom is connected to her in the same manner she is bound to him. She would never choose an apartment as "Our Place" without considering *his* feelings. How could Tom love her and want to live in a home she didn't like? These thoughts make her teary and Tom, grasping the situation, tries to appease her. While wondering why she is so emotional, he reassures her that they will look at other places. They are back from their honeymoon only two days and the first rift between them has already occurred. For the first time, Julie wonders whether Tom really loves her and, doubting her own judgment, whether she really loves him. She pushes these painful thoughts aside as they go on to find an apartment they both like.

As they settle into their new home, Julie and Tom feel more secure about the permanency of their love. In this atmosphere they are free to express themselves spontaneously. At times this self-assertion fits smoothly into, and enhances, their relationship. On some occasions, however, the self-expression of one partner is experienced by the other as a rejection or separation. Tom is a student and spends some evenings studying in the library. Julie's fantasy of marriage to a student includes a picture of her husband studying at home while she works around the house. Tom's behavior does not match Julie's picture and she begins to feel unloved and separated from him. Rather than question the appropriateness of her fantasy, Julie attempts to change Tom to fulfill her image. She does this by expressing her upset and disappointment to Tom, who feels confused and angry. He, in turn, imagines Julie should be grateful for his productive behavior, studying nights in the library in order to get ahead for the family. He does not share Julie's fantasy, judges her as being unreasonable, and believes that if she really loved him, she would understand and reward his sacrifice to study. Tom's logic is persuasive and Julie tries to be more understanding while attempting to overlook her own disappointment and resentment. Tom tries to reassure her of his love but feels vaguely guilty when he goes to the library. He makes an effort to study more at home. The bond between them, once effortlessly loving, is now less secure as each tries to be considerate by holding back feelings and behavior which might threaten their attachment. The honeymoon is over.

EARLY TRAINING:
JULIE AND TOM

Julie was born when her older sister was fifteen. Her mother doted on her, enjoying this opportunity to raise another daughter. Julie's earliest memory is of age three, when her sister was married. She has vivid recollections of the dress she wore and of participating with her mother in the wedding preparations. Sent home from the celebration with an older relative when the hour grew late, Julie could not understand why she had to leave "her wedding." She felt betrayed and disappointed. Family life had always revolved around her. She assumed that the excitement of the wedding also focused on her. She felt punished and had a vague sense that she must have done something wrong. No longer did she feel securely attached to her mother. To protect herself from another disappointment, Julie began to develop tests of her mother's love. She would fantasize that if her mother bought her this toy or that dress, it meant she really loved her. As she increasingly attached her feelings to the desired objects in these tests, her relationship with her mother diminished. The more separated she felt from her mother, the more important these fantasies became.

Tom's younger sister was born when he was two and a half years old. Although he did not recall the events surrounding this birth, he remembered his mother frequently becoming upset, depressed, and anxious. He experienced his mother's depression as a separation and attempted to reunite by behaving as he thought she expected him to behave. Because his mother's condition was generally not contingent on his conduct, his efforts to reconnect were usually frustrated. He became unusually self-reliant and tried to gain attention and approval by becoming effective at various tasks. His attachment to his mother was ultimately characterized by a sense of guilt and helplessness when she became upset, for which he tried to compensate by feeling effective in his accomplishments. In place of an actual positive relationship with this parent, he substituted a fantasy of becoming successful and eventually caring for her.

Julie and Tom are disguised names for a couple who came into couples psychotherapy four months after their wedding. You may have guessed that their complaints were a fear of separation, feelings of hurt and disappointment that neither partner lived up to the fantasy of the other, and anxiety mixed with depression over the inability to pursue their respective interests without feeling criticized and rejected. As children both Julie and Tom were reared in a manner that led to the development of inordinately strong beliefs that they could eventually fulfill their desires if they behaved well. Seldom were they told that their wishes could or would not be granted. Their respective parents had difficulty admitting their limitations to provide all that was sought after. Instead, they helped lead their children into believing that they eventually could have anything they wanted—if only they were good! Although somewhat extreme, Julie and Tom's coupling has the paradoxical elements inherent in all loving relationships.

RECAPITULATING CHILDHOOD THEMES

When we fall in love, we attribute the loftiest motives and highest ideals to our mate. All that was positive in our view of the mothering environment is assigned to our lover. This replication of the early mother–child intimacy is necessary for the formation of a loving relationship. The idealized picture of this connection is relatively fixed. However, we continue to change, as we did in childhood, and require a constant shift in how we relate in order to sustain our happiness. We are in a tug of war. We want to hold on to the excitement and passion associated with our love while we adjust to the reality of daily living. The discrepancy between our changing needs and our idealized image of marriage contains the seeds for much discord and pain. We face this struggle in a style similar to that of our childhood. We recapitulate, albeit modified, the essential themes of our early parent–child relationship. It is amazing that in the face of overwhelming evidence that our idealized marital construct is unrealistic, we persist in our attempts to maintain this picture.

DEVELOPING FANTASIES

Fantasized expectations are developed when a child's needs go unmet. At such times the child may be cranky, demanding, and sullen. Parents generally become anxious and upset at such behavior and try to stop it. One method to alter a child's unpleasant reaction is to promise some future reward in exchange for desirable conduct. "Don't cry, Daddy will buy you ice cream," is a common response to a child's tears. The youngster shifts attention from the felt deprivation to the future reward. He or she trusts the parent and maintains attachment by altering his or her conduct. This sacrifice of spontaneity is associated with the image of a loving parent giving the reward. This image takes on the force of a positive link to a loving parent at a time when the youngster feels helpless and alone in attempting to gratify himself or herself. As he or she grows, the child's needs become more complex. The child's inability to fulfill these wants becomes increasingly painful. To alleviate this pain and to control undesirable actions, parents spell out more and more images of how the child will achieve contentment at a later time. These images ultimately develop into an organized conditional picture of, "If only I stop (begin) that behavior which makes my parent upset (content), I can have my prize." The formation of these constructs is not necessarily consciously provided by the parent. Having their own needs and fantasies, parents frequently act in such a fashion as to transmit nonverbally (for example, through a smile or frown) their unconscious expectations of programmed behavior to their children. Those anticipations of forthcoming love for good conduct scripted into the child's consciousness become a fantasy and reference for future expectations. They also help to mold the youngster's actions to parental standards. The child renounces spontaneous behavior in order to feel part of a loving family.

Almost everyone has fantasies. Through our imagination we can be close to people, places, and times that often are beyond our reach in reality. It is this ability to make us seem positively attached that makes fantasy such a powerful experience. We all fear separation, alienation, and loneliness, and developing an active fantasy life can help us overcome this fear and pain of separateness. However, when our fantasies become so fixed and vivid that we substitute them for a loving relationship, we lose sight of our goal. We can enjoy neither our images nor our actual partners.

DEALING WITH NEGATIVE EFFECTS OF FANTASIES

One way that the negative effects of fantasies can be overcome is through a series of bridging experiences when actually separated from a loved one. Newlyweds, for example, must face the reality that they cannot constantly remain together. They must work, market, and do errands apart. A common bridging experience is for couples to exchange anecdotes of daily events upon reuniting. Even though they cannot spend all their time in exclusivity, everyday occurrences are interesting happenings to be invested in the marriage. Each partner can experience the singular aspects of living as material to enhance the union. Even apart, each can think of the other. The separation is balanced by the quality of closeness when united.

Similarly, children learn to tolerate separations from their loving parents through a variety of bridging experiences. The young child plays peekaboo and acquires a sense of attachment to the unseen adult. Intertwined with being absorbed in playing with blocks, the youngster calls to mother to see his or her "house." Little children can often be seen carrying on a solitary conversation with an absent parent. Likewise, parents develop ways of remaining attached to their young while disunited. Mothers can read a magazine or prepare a meal while at the same time rocking a carriage or crib. If mother goes shopping, she may purchase a toy to bring home. What mother is not so connected to her own that she cannot distinguish from a cacophony of calls to hear her particular "Ma"? This sensitive heedfulness to each other serves as the training ground for feelings of security even when apart from loved ones.

ATTRIBUTING POWER TO THE LOVED ONE

Throughout the courtship and early days of marriage, each time lovers are joined they feel better than when apart. These accumulated and reinforced experiences lead each spouse to associate this elated state with his or her mate. Since neither can make himself or herself feel as good elsewhere, both ascribe the power to bring this happy condition about to their mate. Whether it is termed "chemistry," "my other half brings out the best in me," or "he (or she) lights up my life," there is no doubt that people in love attribute their heightened well-being to a power possessed by their lover. The separations necessitated by daily living further reinforce this notion of the mate's power, since no other relationship comes close to generating such intense pleasure. Each member of the dyad comes to look forward to, and depend upon, the other to make him or her feel happy. In a society that is increasingly depersonalized, where imperviousness to our individuality is experienced daily, and in a world where computers and programmed pathways take precedence over human concerns, our need and hunger for a direct pronouncement of our value and worth become more urgent. As technology becomes more important in influencing the quality of our lives, the need for intimate, loving relationships becomes more desperate. Attributing to our marital partner the power to make us happy places a heavier burden on him or her. The combination of an alienated society and increased pressure on couples to overcome this sense of detachment is part of the reason our divorce rate is so high. During The Honeymoon Is Over stage of becoming a couple, both partners must surpass this hurdle if the marriage is to develop.

This identification of potency to bring about well-being is akin to the child's perception of the loving parent. The youngster rarely feels more gratified than when held in his or her mother's lap and sung to softly while being stroked. Despite a multitude of needs, the state of greatest pleasure is a positive attachment to a loving parent. This becomes reinforced by experiences in separation. What young child doesn't go running to mother when he or she falls and is hurt? What loving mother does not offer solace and comfort when her offspring comes crying with, "Tommy hit me"? No one is more personally concerned, caring, or sensitive to the specific needs of a child than his or her loving parent. The power to make the baby or young child feel happy and secure is part of a parent's motivation. This mutually supported and reinforced interaction between parent and child gives increased credence to the belief that another person has the power to make us happy. When we mature we bring this belief to our loving relationship.

DEALING WITH DISAPPOINTMENT

When Julie and Tom began couples therapy, they both had unquestioned faith in the power of each to please the other. In fact, their chief criticism of each other was that they were not behaving in a manner that would recreate the early state of euphoria experienced prior to their honeymoon. Rather than question whether they possessed such ability, they both concluded that the absence of this behavior meant that their partner no longer cared for them. They reasoned that since they had once experienced such an all-pervasive loving feeling, their partner must have the power to recreate this condition. They both felt their disappointment and hurt was caused by their mate. Both became anxious and, in their insecurity, regressed to a response learned previously when they felt like a bad child. Each partner became a critical parent and a bad child to the other. At that point a detachment occurred, with both partners withdrawn, hurt, angry, and disappointed.

Julie and Tom's disappointment is common to most new-lyweds. This disappointment is often met with confusion and fear. The expectation that our mate will always support us, that the power to elevate our lowered spirits rests with our beloved, to be called forth for our personal use when needed, now has to be questioned. Curiously, we rarely doubt the force or desire of our mate to bolster our sagging self-image. In the early phase of marriage, the interdependency of the pair is so structured as to maintain the illusion that each partner possesses the strength and ability to function as a good mothering parent. To doubt our mate's capacity to render such fulfillment is to jeopardize our belief that we are engaged in a unity designed to produce a state of euphoria unlike any other relationship. Rather than question our spouse's ability or intent, we invariably blame ourselves for the resultant disharmony. Believing our partner's love for us can repair any damage to our egos, we set about seeking ways of eliciting this love. Instead of pleasing our companion because it pleases us, we try to gratify our mate in order to manipulate him or her to restore the lost state of bliss. Something we have done wrong or not done right has to be altered to keep our original fantasy intact. In the early stage of marital development this focus on behavioral change is generally perceived as an opportunity for self-improvement. We usually assume that the criticism and lack of support from our spouse comes from a benevolent source. This perception may, indeed, be in consonance with our own evaluation and could spur us on to develop better skills for living. We try harder.

LOSS OF UNCONDITIONAL LOVE

However, the damage is done. We can no longer believe in unconditional love. There is a crack in the symbiosis. We cannot count completely on our mate to respond according to our wishes. There is a difference between us in the way we perceive situations of conflict. This difference in perception is usually experienced as undesirable, as a threat to our picture of romantic love. Our very effort to repair this damage is further evidence that we are not as one. The necessity to change ourselves in order to accommodate another proves we are deficient. The feeling of lost love and accompanying disjointedness in our marriage make us anxious. This discomfort and insecurity lead to our increased dependence on our mate to restore our debilitated self-image.

Unhappy children turn to their loving parent for reassurance and succor. Past experiences have led them to expect such a response. When physical or emotional injury was received, the mothering one found some way to restore the broken body or ego. The parent's identification with the child's needs was so complete as to offer aid and explanation in accord with the youngster's view of the situation. The first time a loving parent responds to his or her offspring's complaints with criticism usually disorients the child. There is a rift in the symbiotic tie: they are no longer as one. This is more of a threat to the youngster than the injury brought to the parent. In an attempt to reestablish the former alliance, the child alters his or her perception of the painful event to coincide with that of the mothering parent. The insecurity and fear of losing the mother's love shakes the child's confidence in his or her own perceptions and judgments, leading to a reappraisal of the child's outlook. If he or she can learn to present hurts in a fashion that meets with the mother's approval, the child can continue to feel positively connected. To do this, however, the child must increase dependency on her perceptions at the expense of developing individual insights. If the parent's orientation is consistent with the child's encounters with reality, the child easily adopts this outlook and develops successful skills to deal with problems in living. If the parental views are discordant with the youngster's experiences, however, the youngster renounces his or her own perceptions, withdraws from the painful encounters, and increases the dependency on the parent.

During the first four years of life, differences in perception between child and parent generally leave the child more dependent on the parent's outlook and values. These differences further lead to the experience of separateness between the two and a corresponding attempt to realign the child's behavior to gain parental approval. The youngster adopts the attitudes and actions specified by the loving parent. He or she tries harder to be good.

Newlyweds tend to react to a blow to their expectations with the personality and character structure developed early in life. The character, or habitual style of dealing with problems of living, is fairly well formed at maturity. Throughout the formative years of development, those repetitious patterns of behavior that lead to the greatest success and avoid the most discomfort become incorporated into an organized system of functioning which is synonymous with our self-image. This system is generally so fixed by adulthood that our actions are an identifiable and predictable statement of who we are. When our security is threatened, we tend to fall back on earlier modes of behavior which are associated with greater safety. This regression, which generally leads to a temporary stability in the threatened relationship, takes place at the expense of spontaneous expressiveness. It is cautious behavior designed to avoid trouble. Being on guard, and highly sensitive to the reactions of one another, the recently formed couple begin to search for ways to remain positively united while striving for authentic self-expression. This is often difficult work for most pairs.

LOSS OF FANTASY

The attempt to avoid arousing the critical parent in each other tends to direct most spouses to a greater awareness of their mate's true identity. Where previously fantasy and expectation prevailed, an appreciation, understanding, and acceptance of the real personalities of each partner now begin to become possible. If the actual make-up of each mate is not at too great a variance with the spouse's expectations, this learning process can be a smooth one. However, if the fantasy of either one or both members of the coupling is inordinately different from their mate's personality, trouble can be expected. A basic problem all couples face is how to display and expose their authentic selves without causing a critical parent reaction in each other. In the formative years of a marriage the tendency is to mask that true identity which gives rise to disapproval. Although this helps to minimize conflict, it makes it virtually impossible to be spontaneous or to enable the spouse to learn how to become effective with the authentic personality of his or her mate. A series of gradual, cautious trade-offs usually ensues, with the spouse revealing the least offensive qualities while watching closely the mate's reactions. If the response is an accepting one, further revelations will be forthcoming. If not, a period of consolidation takes place where the offensive trait is kept hidden. Attempts to alter this trait within oneself are balanced with efforts to get the mate to accept the previously rejected behavior. Thus, a little self-exposure, along with efforts at self-improvement and an exertion to change one's partner to accept one as one is, combine to form the style of marriage.

GETTING STUCK

Through such trial and error, couples learn to compromise individual needs in order to maintain a balance of reasonable closeness. However, there are some behaviors for which no compromise is possible because they have been experienced in early childhood as essential for survival. If a child learns that criticism of his or her mother renders her anxious, helpless, and totally unavailable, that child will withdraw rather than openly express resentment. This characteristic behavior becomes nonnegotiable. In a later love relationship that individual will withdraw when feeling resentment. His or her loving partner experiences this withdrawal as a rejection but has no idea of the cause, or even if it is meant for him or her. If, in turn, the loving partner's early experience was characterized by abandonment through death or divorce of the parents, this partner will find the other's withdrawal intolerable. He or she will feel panic and instinctively search for a way to reunite. The harder the loving partner tries, the more the other withdraws. Tears and tantrums do not work. In desperation the loving partner threatens to leave. Faced with this threat of separation, the other finally reaches out. When the reunion takes place, both partners experience intense relief and feel strongly attached. However, a pattern is set which will be replayed endlessly. The marriage is volatile, as neither partner can control his or her response to the primitive anxiety originating in childhood that is automatically set off by the mate.

When such a condition characterizes a marital relationship, the couple will find it extremely difficult to develop beyond The Honeymoon Is Over phase of marriage. The fixated pattern of response is too deeply entrenched to be readily changed. Such couples struggle in circles to get beyond their pain. The ensuing despair and impotence often lead to a dissolution of the marriage. Not surprisingly, however, subsequent attempts at sustaining a loving relationship with a new partner also fail. Rather than perceiving their pattern of interaction as the problem, such individuals generally tend to blame their mate for their unhappiness.

Getting stuck at The Honeymoon Is Over phase of marriage is not an infrequent occurrence. Young couples, especially, tend to adhere to their fantasies of romantic love. Compromising their ideals or altering their expectations of "living happily ever after" is experienced as a defeat or betrayal. These newlyweds can spend years attempting to change each other to match their respective pictures of happiness. In the course of such efforts, many creative and ingenious methods are devised to influence the marital style. Sometimes the changing patterns of marriage bring a temporary excitement or passion to the couple that encourages them to continue their search for fantasy fulfillment. To outsiders they look like the "perfect pair."

Friends and family are astonished when such a couple decides to separate. No one can understand how such a split can take place. Yet it is precisely this adherence to their fantasies that ultimately defeats this couple. No marriage can indefinitely sustain itself on the energy generated by fantasy. Unless a couple begins to move toward an awareness, understanding, and acceptance of their true personhoods, the marriage is not likely to succeed.

WORKING OUT HARMONY

The time spent from about seven years of age to adolescence in suppressing one's impulses for the expected fulfillment of a loving relationship makes it particularly difficult for young people to relinquish their fantasies. All those years of deprivation and self-sacrifice are invested with the self-righteous belief in the goal of romantic love. The images and constructs of love that evolved during this time have an enormous force of their own. The passion and intensity of such love further reinforce the validity of the fantasies incorporating these feelings. Young people are not likely to give up such treasures too easily. What they need is to maintain their marital relationship while buying time to mellow and evolve the skills for close interpersonal ties. Too often, however, the impetuousness of youth leads to an irreconcilable break in an otherwise potentially fruitful marriage. The ability to continue relating to a partner while asserting oneself is a skill originating in childhood.

Children attempt to sustain a loving connection to their parents as they become more self-assertive. When behavior meets with parental rejection, the child's initial response is to disown the actions. "I can't help it—Tommy made me do it" is often heard amid promises that the offense will never be committed again. If the critical act reflects the child's personality or if the reality of his or her environment continues to generate such conduct, the child either must learn to hide this behavior or succeed in gaining acceptance where previously there was rejection. The young child is not capable of self-approval in the face of parental criticism. If the family's standards are inordinately in conflict with the child's needs, the behavior is most likely to become covert and the youngster will grow with a sense of secrecy about him. The child will also most likely identify his or her hidden behavior as bad.

Most youngsters, however, learn to intertwine hiding and self-exposure with efforts to gain parental acceptance of their behavior. They manage to keep a balance between family closeness and self-exploration. Sometimes, humor is employed to share an outrageous act. At an early age, children learn that cute facial expressions evoke adult laughter. It is not unusual for a young child to do that which is forbidden or to deny a wrongdoing with a smile of innocence designed to ward off parental disapproval. Also, soliciting the opinion of parents about a social situation frequently brings the two together. Reporting on the behavior of a friend is another way of exploring parental attitudes. Through these, and a host of other methods, children develop the skills to experiment with their own life styles while remaining within the family fold. The family's value system and the child's efforts to gain approval for his or her natural expressiveness blend into the resultant habitual stylized manner of interpersonal behavior. It is this characteristic pattern which is later applied in attempts to accommodate a marital partner.

The skills a child develops to accommodate parents while evolving an individual personality do not necessarily work with a marital partner. Despite some similarities, marriage partners are not our parents. It is the *process* of working out a way to live harmoniously while expressing oneself that is important. Specific behavioral traits and patterns have limited value both for ourselves and our spouses. To continue to explore oneself and discover untapped resources is one of the greatest joys of living. Remaining fixed in particular modes of being narrows both the quality and intensity of our pleasure. To insist on demanding acceptance for our behavior, no matter how benevolently intended, is to invite disaster. Disappointments occur in marriage as partners unsuccessfully try to please their mates according to their own fantasies. Julie buys Tom an expensive gift for his birthday because she would be pleased with such a present. Tom is resentful of the expense. He tries to manage the budget economically because he thinks Julie will feel more secure and be pleased by this display of caring. She, in turn, feels hurt, perceiving him as withholding. Expressions meant as love and concern continue to be seen as rejections. Repeated efforts to please do not result in a loving connection. Each spouse feels cheated and self-righteous. Each begins to blame the other for the unhappiness, as resentment turns to anger. Scores are kept and a power struggle ensues. Interspersed with attempts to get their own way, the couple engage more and more in retaliatory behavior. If they cannot obtain what they want from their mate, they can certainly make this partner miserable. Since the honeymoon is indeed over, they now engage in Getting Even.

3

chapter

GETTING EVEN

Pam and Brian have been together for five years. Their marriage, shaky from the beginning, included a trial separation of several months. The disconnection was too painful, motivating them to try again. Their attempts to negotiate a more comfortable living arrangement, however, continually bump into the same basic issues. Brian's fantasy of a loving marriage depicts his wife as always wanting sex, wishing to be with him constantly, and desiring to please him. He does not get along with Pam's family and wants to limit the time spent with them. Pam's fantasy of a loving relationship is an understanding husband who shares her desire for family closeness, is supportive of her difficulties at work, accepting of her need for privacy, and undemanding of her sexually. Brian presses for more closeness while Pam pushes against him for more space.

Brian's anxiety over separateness dictates a need for structure. If Pam goes out, he feels more comfortable knowing when she will return. If they visit her family, he is able to relax only when they have pre-arranged a specific time to leave. With this format he is able to live more in the present. Pam, on the other hand, becomes anxious with structure. If she is committed to departing at a particular time, her ability to function in the here and now is limited. She feels pressured by having to watch the clock. When Brian expresses anger at Pam's lateness, she retaliates by making additional social plans. Brian counters by staying out late for several nights. When they try to talk, matters get worse. Pam thinks Brian's urgings for togetherness are self-centered. Brian interprets her need for more space as a rejection. They frequently maintain this war-like state for several days. When the hurt and loneliness become intolerable, they somehow manage to get together. They reassure each other of their love and are happy for a short time. Usually, the bubble bursts when Brian initiates a sexual move which Pam perceives as a demand. She feels taken advantage of. She has already given of herself lovingly and it is never enough. She backs away, refusing Brian's overture. He feels hurt. Since they were so close only moments before, the rejection and disappointment are all the more painful.

What starts out as a loving interaction is converted into a power struggle. Both partners define love in terms of what the other does for them. Each seeks happiness in accordance with a private fantasy and reacts to the other with defiance. If, after a pleasant dinner, Pam asks for help with the dishes, Brian responds with, "When you can come home on time, I'll help you around the house." His stipulations infuriate her. She is positive his only motive is to control her. This makes her determined to be her own person. Despite her fatigue, she stays up to watch television when he asks her to come to bed. When Brian is attentive and considerate, Pam is suspicious. At precisely those times he wants to be near her, she remembers she has a call to make. His tenderness is often reacted to with, "This will get you nowhere. I don't want sex tonight." It is rare to find them expressing warmth at the same time. Yet there is no doubt that there is a profound tie between them.

Pam and Brian are using each other to act out their internal conflicts. When Pam is unavailable, Brian becomes aware of his dependence on her. This frightens him. He overreacts by becoming angry and demanding. If he were able to accept his need, Pam would be more responsive. Pam is also struggling against her dependency. She wants to please Brian and get close to him but is frightened and overwhelmed by intimacy. If she could display her fear instead of pushing him away, he, too, would be more understanding. Both react to their vulnerability by trying to control the other, thus escalating their tension. The resulting power struggle polarizes them further until they are forced to distance themselves. However, neither can tolerate being apart too long. Their mutual dependency leads to a cautious friendliness. They make tentative gestures to please each other and the cycle begins anew.

Couples who become locked into a power struggle are putting their energy into trying to control each other. They are continually defending against their own vulnerability and helplessness through attempts at mastering the relationship. They experience their mate as a critical parent and, consequently, each feels like a bad child. Because they use their power negatively, they reinforce their feelings of guilt. Their sensitivity to their partner's endeavors to control them limits their options to respond. They are relegated to one stance—"You can't tell me what to do." Frequently, the very qualities which cause such explosiveness were once perceived as attractive. What Pam now sees as demanding she once judged as strength. Brian seemed sure of himself and what he wanted. His craving for her made Pam feel loved and beautiful. Brian initially considered Pam's fear of intimacy as desirable. He was unexcited by aggressive women and drawn to Pam's apparent shyness and uncertainty. He felt strong and she felt wanted.

EARLY TRAINING: PAM AND BRIAN

Pam is the second of four children. She recalls a harried mother endlessly scurrying to care for her offspring. Pam wanted and sought attention while feeling ashamed of herself. When Pam got upset, her mother became anxious. This frightened Pam and led to a shift in focus from herself to her mother. To maintain this parent as strong, Pam tried to appear the self-contained child she thought her mother wanted her to be. In order to look happy, she suppressed her feelings of deprivation. She grew up judging her own needs as bad and wrong. Pam's childhood experience taught her that closeness means becoming what the other person wants. Although she desperately desires intimacy, she is constantly afraid of losing herself in an intimate relationship. Pam's need to have others define her leads to her feeling torn between Brian and her family. She is afraid to displease either. Fear thus becomes a pressure which she finds intolerable. She is caught between feeling frightened to relate and afraid of loneliness. Her passion is expressed most intensely in the power struggle. Although this is ungratifying, such emotionality validates her sense of self.

Brian grew up an only child. His mother, deprived and unsatisfied in her marriage, turned her warmth to him. He was indulged and doted on, quickly learning that when he was anxious, his mother was there for reassurance. Without siblings to dilute the intensity of this relationship, his life seemed complete. He had no need to reach out to other children. All ended abruptly the first day his mother took him to kindergarten and left. He felt betrayed and abandoned. Not knowing how to relate to his classmates, he was afraid of them and tried to leave. With many promises, his mother induced him to remain in school. However, the violation of trust had left its toll. No longer could Brian count on his mother to love him as in the past. Despite his loneliness, he sought gratification through academic achievements. In college he was able to relate on an intellectual level, sharing ideas and perceptions. When he met Pam, Brian's yearning for an exclusive loving relationship reawakened. He centered his life around her and assumed she would do the same. He was certain that his willingness to devote himself to his wife was enough to make the marriage a happy one. However, he lost track of the reality that there was another person on the other end of the relationship who did not share his fantasy.

The intense romanticism of lovers rarely extends beyond two and a half years. For the most part, the initial passion and excitement of a loving relationship begins to wane after six months. Young people, particularly, find this difficult to accept. Understandably, they want such happiness to continue indefinitely. It does not occur to them to seek alternative ways of relating which may be equally rewarding. Instead, the typical couple strive to recreate their romanticism. Our culture does not readily provide acceptable role models for unpassionate couples. The media, generally, present young romantic kinships as the paradigm for loving relationships while frequently making fun of all other styles of marriage. This, along with a host of other societal pressures, adds to a yearning to reexperience that feeling associated with our first love. Believing that the magic of love rests with their mate, young marrieds first try to please each other in order to release this force. When this does not work, they generally turn to criticism and guilt invocation in an attempt to stir their partner. While attacking each other and defending themselves may be an outlet for their unrequited ardor, it does not elicit the desired result. Blaming their spouse for stubbornly withholding love, they become resentful. In this phase of marriage, the energy of the coupling shifts to getting even.

THE POWER STRUGGLE

Failing to reestablish the early loving relationship in The Honeymoon Is Over stage of marriage, couples generally relate through a power struggle in the Getting Even phase. The power struggle is characterized by trying to get our own way, by refusing to submit to our mate's wishes, by unilaterally redefining the rules of the marriage, or by a combination of these. The energy and passion are still invested in the relationship. The power struggle is designed to manipulate our mate into the desired position in our fantasy. Despite the seeming emphasis on self-assertion, the sought-after result is basically a reflection of our wish for dependency fulfillment. We are caught in the paradox of defining our marital happiness through our need to change our partner to take care of us "properly." We are dependent on our spouse's cooperation in this endeavor. When it is not voluntarily forthcoming, we try to force it out of our mate. Predictably, even when we are successful, we are not satisfied. Who wants love if we have to extricate it from our lover? It is valuable only if given freely. Besides, how satisfying can our need for caring be if we must act with determination and forcefulness to obtain it?

In the Getting Even phase of marriage we punish our mate for not relating to us as *we* are. We want a relationship—but one that centers around our concept of closeness. All day long we relate to others principally as they are. We accommodate to our environment. Whether we want something from someone or desire to serve another, we must think, act, and speak as the established traditions and rules dictate as proper. We want to relate effortlessly to our spouse—but we also wish this partner to reach out to us. When both members of the dyad want to be cared for at the same time, disappointment and struggle are inevitable. The wish to be connected to our marital partner in terms of our own needs has its roots in our parent–child relationship.

Having experienced the loss of the symbiotic tie, the young child renounces spontaneity in order to please the mothering one. However, this does not bring unconditional love. The child becomes more attentive to the standards of this parent and behaves in a fashion he or she believes will gratify. This, too, does not recreate the early attachment. The resultant hurt and frustration are used to motivate the mothering one to feel sorrow, compassion, and sympathy for the child's wants. Success in this situation usually is short lived. The youngster soon finds himself or herself again disconnected from the loving parent. By the fourth year of life, when a child's grandiosity reaches its peak, the youngster pits self against the parents. The youngster wants his or her own way while insisting that dependency needs continue to be met. A power struggle takes place. The idyllic parent–child relationship is replaced by a battle of nerves. Children blame and attack their parents. Parents criticize and punish their children. Each tries to mold the other to comply with their respective image of proper role behavior. Eventually, the youngster's dependency forces him or her to submit. The youngster does so, however, still believing that he or she can obtain the early loving connection.

Once a spouse feels he or she has done all possible to rejuvenate a sagging marriage, he or she begins to blame the mate for their troubles. Resentment turns to anger. Feeling self-righteous and victimized, the spouse tries to hurt his or her partner. One way to inflict pain on a mate is to turn to others for emotional satisfaction. Most people have enough friends and acquaintances who will readily support and encourage their formulation of the problem. With such allies, fixed positions can become nonnegotiable basic principles of living. What starts out as a quarrel can take on the proportions of a vendetta. Having an affair, sexual or otherwise, is a device often used by couples to hurt each other. An affair for this purpose takes place when the emotional energy of hurt and anger, along with an emphasis on self-justification, is greater than the investment in the new relationship. The fundamental tie is still to the marital partner. The fulfillment received in the affair primarily serves to reinforce and justify the position taken in the family fight. When one spouse defends his or her anger against the other by referring to the success in a new relationship, you can be sure this spouse's heart is still with the marital partner.

WEAPONS IN THE
POWER STRUGGLE

Children learn to wield power over an unfulfilling parent by turning to others. If they can't get what they want from one, they can seek satisfaction from the other parent. Youngsters are quite perceptive. They quickly grasp an opportunity to play one parent against the other. This is especially true when parents use child-rearing practices as the vehicle for expressing their dissatisfactions with each other. In those homes where mother and father share in developing their offspring's character, the maneuver of playing one parent against the other quickly comes to light. In which case, a grandmother, aunt, or neighbor can be employed to carry on a power struggle with an unrelenting parent. In either example, the mothering one typically becomes indignant and angry over the youngster's success in obtaining his or her wants elsewhere. This usually leads to retaliation by restricting and depriving the child. The strong-willed youngster sometimes will respond by deliberately exposing this parent as ungiving, selfish, and cruel. Invoking guilt in a devoted parent is often sufficient to get one's way temporarily. If nothing else, the astonished adult is also impressed with the child's capacity and daring to compete in this manner. In passive, highly dependent parents, this trait may even be encouraged, albeit unconsciously, as a means of acting out the parent's unfulfilled wishes for self-assertion. However, the child's use of others to obtain gratification is quite limited. His or her dependency need for security ultimately leads to the child's submission to parental control.

Parents, too, use others to influence their offspring. It is not uncommon to hear a parent compare a child to siblings or friends in order to increase control over this youngster. "Come on, eat your spinach. Look how Tommy cleaned his plate" is a frequent invocation to a dawdling youngster. Using the power and influence of each other to discipline is another device used by parents. "If you don't drink your milk, I'll tell your father when he gets home." Threatening children with punishment to be inflicted by unseen others is yet another favorite controlling mechanism. Whether the policeman, teacher, priest, or God, invisible reinforcements readily add to parental power to get a child to comply. When youngsters defy or resist parental control, parents frequently resort to using the authority of others to increase their power. The manner in which this power is employed and the effect it has on the parent–child relationship will set the stage for the child's use of such stratagems in adulthood.

The use of money is another device frequently employed in a couple's power struggle. Money, as a medium of exchange, serves as an interface between the family and society. Who earns money, who spends it, on what and how, with whose consultation or permission, along with when this is done, is often an arena for control. Typically, the husband will hold back money while the wife spends in order to hurt the partner and assert power. The once-generous lover who impulsively spent his week's salary on a date suddenly becomes a tight-fisted miser. The previously frugal and concerned girl-friend who advocated saving and "let's eat in," starts hoarding furs and jewelry. What was once considered "ours" now becomes "mine." Curiously, the advent of working wives and the increased sharing in family support by both spouses has not altered this situation much. While many working wives retain their earnings in a separate account as a means of exerting power and independence in the marriage, economic control of the family is still largely in the male domain. Regardless of who earns the money, couples often convert their marital dissatisfactions into a power struggle over the control of this commodity.

While couples can argue passionately over costs and priorities of expenditures, the attentive listener can detect a more fundamental concern. "Why do you need that dress?" can be a substitute for, "I am hurt and jealous that you seek compliments and attention from other men", or "If you don't give me the love I want, I shall go out and get it myself by having my hair done, buying clothes, and arranging for my own entertainment." When a husband says, "I can't afford it," he often means, "Since you are not treating me the way I expect you to, I am withholding 'my' money from you." When a wife starts running up the family's charge account, she may be trying to tell her husband that she is going to get from him what she wants one way or another. When the control over money becomes a substitute for the expectations in a relationship, it becomes part of the Getting Even phase of becoming a couple.

During the years from two to five, toys are used chiefly as the interface between the family and the world outside. They are a symbol of parental love and concern, as well as a child's measure of his or her acceptability. Initially, parents offer toys to enhance a child's inquisitiveness and development. They are an expression of the symbiotic tie between the two. Both revel in this interchange. In time, however, toys can become a commodity in the power struggle between parent and child. Parents can offer them as rewards for good behavior, as well as withholding toys as a form of punishment. Children, in turn, can play with their toys contentedly, often sharing with the mothering one their prowess in manipulating these objects; or they can destroy or ignore them, make noise or become so absorbed in their activity that they are oblivious to this parent. From toys, children graduate to exploring other material objects in the home. They know quickly which household articles are prized. To obtain attention, youngsters have the uncanny ability to find just the right table to "paint," a drawer to open, or a chair on which to climb. It is but a short step from here to learn to master money as yet another commodity to employ in bargaining with each other. How these objects are used in the parent–child relationship is carried over into marriage.

Sex is another area where a power struggle can take place. This once-exquisite expression of love becomes a powerful weapon to control during the Getting Even phase of marriage. There is probably no greater disappointment and pain than the sexual rejection of one partner by the other. Offering sex or withholding it as a means to change a mate deprives the couple of one of the fundamental ways of spontaneously expressing themselves. When a pair gets to the point of using sex to hurt each other, they are deeply into a power struggle that may be impossible to resolve.

The function of body elimination is a highly charged emotional area between parent and child. How, where, and when a youngster eliminates can be a source of approval or punishment. Humiliating a child for wetting himself or herself can be devastating. Nothing gets a parent's attention as quickly as a child's demand in public, "Mommy, I have to go." The early expression of this bodily need becomes a prototype of later physical requirements in a mature relationship.

Similarly, food is a frequent tool in a family's power struggle. Going out to dine is generally a loving interchange between a couple. Using this activity as leverage to influence a mate brings it into another sphere. Cooking for a spouse can be an expression of love or a preparation for a demand. Throwing a TV dinner together sloppily can be a statement of resentment and hostility. Once on vacation in St. Thomas, the authors went dancing with a native couple. The wife spent most of the evening complaining that her husband rarely took her out. He countered with, "Everyone knows that a man needs to feel loved by a wife who cooks especially for him." She shot back, "When you treat me like your girl friend, I will cook for you again." Food, as a basic need, is highly susceptible for incorporation into a couple's power struggle.

In the parent–child relationship, food is a fundamental interchange for loving care. Both feel intimately bound by this activity. When the youngster enters the stage of gradiosity at age four, he or she attempts to master this relationship according to individual needs. Refusal to eat is often one way to exercise such control. The mother's need to feel effective in nourishing her young makes her especially vulnerable to such tactics. She, in turn, tends to demand, "Eat, eat, damn it." Such interactions lay the groundwork for the use of food in later power struggles.

Another area for potential power struggles is time. Time, being limited and irreversible, is readily adaptable to contention for control. Getting home on time, being ready for a date, or coming to bed when expected can be sources of gratification or frustration in a marriage. As a couple becomes increasingly accustomed to function within a rhythmical cycle, they are more liable to disappointment and hurt when this sequence is broken. Not living up to the sequence can be a message of rejection or revenge between a couple. This method of getting even leaves the injured party with no recourse for immediate remedy—the time has already passed. Equally frustrating is a series of time disappointments such that a previously accepted understanding can no longer be taken for granted. This unilateral alteration of a family's tempo leaves little room for challenge—except by a similar strategy on the part of the other spouse.

There are many other ways of getting even with a mate who withholds love to frustrate his partner. Excessive drinking, not going to work, remaining in bed all day, getting sick, not filling the gas tank, and innumerable other ploys have been reported to us as a means of inflicting pain on a mate. Perhaps you know of some strategies that are particularly effective in helping to gain mastery over a relationship.

HAZARDS OF THE
GETTING EVEN STAGE

Getting Even is a hazardous stage of marriage. If you are too successful, you will irreparably injure your partner. When hurt is too intense and traumatic, or the frequency of pain does not afford your partner a chance to recuperate, he or she may protect himself or herself by no longer caring. It is not anger or hurt that stops the coupling process: It is *indifference*. There is passion in the power struggle. Trying to get your own way is loaded with excitement and energy. The emotional release in this interchange is intense. Frequently, couples in a power struggle have their most enjoyable sex during this period. If you maintain your focus on relating to your mate, you are not likely to go too far in hurting this partner. When you are joined to a spouse who is hurting, you will feel your spouse's pain and stop. If, however, you make your demands or need for revenge primary, you may not be sensitive enough to refrain from going too far. You may inflict such pain as to cause your partner to become indifferent. An indifferent partner leads to a dead marriage: the cessation of the evolvement of the coupling process. With all the trials and excesses in *Gone with the Wind*, it is not until Rhett Butler tells Scarlett, "Frankly, my dear, I don't give a damn," that the marriage is over.

What is most important to understand during the Getting Even phase of coupling is that the power struggle is a reaction to our sense of impotence. As much as our fantasies dictate that our happiness lies with an unconditionally loving partner, we are, in fact, helpless to bring this about. *No* spouse can continuously live up to our expectations. If we can question our expectations, rather than our mate, we have a better chance of making the marriage work. Attempting to deny our powerlessness to change our spouse, we regress to seeking mastery, control, potency, in our marital relationship. The power struggle is a loser, for if we win, we lose.

Couples are intensely related during the power struggle. Ostensibly, each spouse is affirming individuality, or separateness. In fact, the process can help cement the marriage. In this condition, an extramarital affair is experienced as a terrible threat because it represents a disconnection. It is inconceivable to the one left behind that the partner could cohabit with another and still be connected to him or her. The one having the affair experiences it as an affirmation of separateness. Seen thus, the primary relationship is still the marriage.

When Pam says, "I need more space," she is expressing her connectedness. When she physically separates, the space becomes threatening to her, and she reaches out to pull Brian back. In the emptiness, she has lost her definition of herself. In the connection, however, she defines herself in reaction to him. This process is paralleled in the developing child from the ages of two to five. The growing child starts to define self in terms of what he or she is not. When the child says "no," he or she is beginning to separate from the mother by saying "that is not me." It is a long journey from "that is not me" to "this is who I am." Many people, particularly women, never grow out of a negative self-definition. Women, more than men, grow up with a self-concept that is the negative of their mothers'. Curiously, this apparently independent stance is, in fact, an expression of dependence. As long as a woman says, "I am not like my mother," she is her mother's daughter. If she were to define herself independently, she would, in effect, be her own authority. She could no longer sustain an image of herself as someone's daughter. Many women substitute husband for mother as their authority. Their dependence, as well as their resentment and defiance, is transferred from mother to husband, keeping their childish position intact. It is easier for a boy to identify himself positively while separating from his mother.

To break out of the reactive circle is extremely difficult and with some couples, impossible. When Pam is with Brian, her focus shifts to him. Then, she does not want what he demands of her. If they separate and she is surrounded by a larger space, she is able to become aware that it is Brian she wants. If they get back together, her focus again shifts to him and she becomes reactive. At some point, the emotional intensity becomes exhausting, the threat of separation becomes too frightening, and both start to shift their focus from each other to the environment. They become engaged in one or more mutually gratifying activities enabling them to hang in and solidify their connection.

4
chapter

HANGING IN

Wendy and David have been married nine years. They have a five-year-old daughter. Wendy became pregnant when her relationship with David was marked by much friction. Although the pregnancy was unplanned, it seemed to distract them from an endless series of power struggles. The prospect of having a baby provided some excitement for them both. It afforded each a different perspective on themselves and their marriage.

In the early years of marriage, Wendy worked as a teacher while David was a graduate sociology student. Wendy was phobic about separations. During their first year together, she clung to David, telephoning him several times a day. She constantly needed to know where he was and when he would be home. David felt pressured by her inordinate attachment and was critical of her clinging. In her eagerness to please, Wendy tried to overcome her anxiety and behave in a less demanding manner. She took courses at night to keep herself busy. When she became somewhat successful at separating from David, she found herself attracted to another graduate student. Although contact with the other man was limited to several conversations a week, Wendy felt both excited and guilty about this new relationship. She shared these feelings with David, who became threatened, hurt, and angry. He reacted by suggesting a separation. Wendy panicked, promised it would never happen again, and put her energy into reassuring David of her devotion to him.

During the next few years, quarrels were more frequent. Generally, they revolved around Wendy's desire to socialize and party. She wanted to share her excitement with David. Although David enjoyed his wife's vitality and enthusiasm, his distrust of her reactions to other men made mixing in public painful. He wanted to keep Wendy's excitement within the confines of their relationship. Wendy, in turn, found increasing difficulty in providing stimulation for the marriage, since there was little spontaneity from David. She also felt too frightened and insecure to attempt socializing by herself. Predictably, their power struggles took the form of each threatening to hurt the other by her having an affair or by his leaving. Wendy's pregnancy presented a temporary solution to their marital dilemma. It helped both feel more secure about the strength of their connection and provided an excitement that did not threaten their marriage.

When their daughter was a year old, Wendy became restless. Her roles of wife and mother were too limiting. She began to talk of returning to school. About this time, David secured a well-paying job at a distant university. They decided to buy a house in their new location. Wendy put aside her desire to return to school and invested her energies into fixing and furnishing her new home. As her daughter grew, Wendy's involvement in the community deepened. She began to form strong relationships which gradually took her away from home. When she was beginning to feel an integral part of the community, Wendy thought about going back to work. David felt threatened by this display of independence and talked her into staying home to attend to their daughter's needs. Notwithstanding some misgivings, Wendy shifted her focus back to the home.

Despite what seems a successful marriage to outsiders, Wendy and David have never resolved their essential problems. In addition to wrangling about their social life, they disagree about disciplining their daughter, furnishing their home, and arguing. David withdraws, and Wendy shudders at the distance between them. Wendy's attraction to other men is a signal that the ways in which she and David have been holding their marriage together are no longer adequate.

In the early days of their marriage, David's reaction to Wendy's interest in other men reinforced her guilt and self-image as a bad child. Her attempts to reassure David replayed an old script of trying to appease an angry parent. This only heightened her dependency on him. While Wendy worked she had outside sources of approval and positive feedback. This gave her leverage to cope with the bad-child feelings evoked by David. The intensified marital disharmony was proportionate to her increased confidence and self-worth, enabling her to fight more vigorously with David without being overwhelmed by guilt. David's lack of self-confidence was evidenced by the ease with which he was threatened by Wendy's outside interests. His need to feel powerful was principally supplied by his wife's dependency on him. David needed Wendy to rely on him, while Wendy needed David to be strong. They were mutually interdependent. However, their style of marriage made it difficult to face this fact effectively. They both required more positive individuation before they could confront this issue. Having a baby afforded them time and experience to hang in, in the marriage, while each garnered additional personal resources to apply to their coupling.

Becoming pregnant helped Wendy balance her dependence on David with feeling effective as a mother. The shared excitement of parenthood renewed their encouragement for a potentially happy marriage. Having a baby enabled them to hang in by shifting their mutual focus onto something they both created. In time, it also made more manifest Wendy's childlike attachment to David as a parent figure. Wendy's roles as mother and wife dominated her identity after the baby was born. For a while, she no longer felt effective outside her family. This made David's rejection and withdrawal more devastating—a condition she had to correct.

David experienced Wendy's shift to the family as reassuring. While beginning to feel more confident at work, he welcomed his new identity as a parent. The same forces that facilitated Wendy's attachment to him as a child brought to the foreground David's acceptance of his own authority and power. As Wendy's dependency became more apparent, David began to accept *his* need for her. As his self-confidence grew, he could more openly tell Wendy how much he relied on her. Both partners found strength to face their own need. Even if solutions were not readily forthcoming, they could better handle their problem. For both Wendy and David the period of Hanging In—watching their daughter grow and making a home together—represented a positive investment that confirmed the bond between them.

EARLY TRAINING:
WENDY AND DAVID

Wendy's parents were divorced when she was ten. Her father had custody of her. She was eleven years old before her mother was granted visiting rights. Wendy experienced the separation as a punitive abandonment. Although she did not know why, Wendy remembers being careful not to talk about her father while with her mother. Reuniting with her mother, which Wendy had yearned for throughout the severance, was a big disappointment. The reality of irregular visits strained these contacts between mother and daughter. There were countless rules to remember: "Don't touch this," "Boots belong in the closet," and "Doesn't your father teach you manners?" were typical admonitions. She resented her mother's attempts to control her and was terrified of her anger. The relationship always felt tenuous. At any moment she could be told the visit was ended. Every departure was a potential abandonment. Yet her mother clearly loved and wanted her. She took pride in Wendy, showing her off at every opportunity. Mother and daughter spent Christmas and summers together. When Wendy opted to spend part of her vacation elsewhere, her mother was visibly shaken. They shared many interests. Wendy particularly enjoyed helping to furnish her mother's apartment. She also liked fussing with and fixing her mother's hair. Most of this shared time was spent joyfully. Mother and daughter repeatedly spoke of living together when Wendy got older. Any mention, however, of her father or intimate friends led to strong emotional outbursts. It was David's apparent stability and understanding of her fears and anxieties that attracted Wendy. He was supportive in her quarrels with her mother and comforting in her distress. They were married after a short courtship, despite her mother's disapproval.

David was one of two siblings, with a brother ten years his junior. His mother, being unsure of herself, was chronically anxious. He remembers his childhood as joyless. His father died when he was twelve and his mother turned to him as the man in the family. In one fell swoop he lost both parents and his childhood. Although he was unprepared for such a heavy responsibility, David learned to suppress his own fears in order to alleviate his mother's anxiety. In addition to being a good student, he worked part time. All his earnings were contributed to the family. He had practically no social life, for his energies were devoted to school and family. When David was sixteen, his mother announced one evening that she planned to remarry the following week. He felt shocked and betrayed. David was not even aware that his mother had a boyfriend. When he met Wendy, David was quickly responsive to her emotionality and felt effective in his efforts to protect her. He was happy at the prospect of being in control of his own family destiny.

Both Wendy and David were deprived of affection as children. Each developed potent fantasies of a loving spouse.

Wendy's insecurity and fear of abandonment make emotional distance especially painful. Her attraction to other men reinforces her security needs by helping her feel desired and wanted. When she withholds her feelings from David, she fantasizes being free with other men. Her inability to tolerate separation, however, keeps her from acting out these wishes. She is controlled by her own need for reassurance but experiences this restraint as coming from David. This combination keeps the relationship volatile. David, in turn, requires a faithful companion. Since he perceives all his emotional needs as being met by his family, he cannot understand Wendy's desire for others. His self-image as the all-fulfilling mate is threatened by his wife's outside interests. While he finds it burdensome to restrict her, his fantasy of a loving couple prevents him from sharing in Wendy's social longings. Both feel relieved and reassured when they conjointly participate in a mutual interest.

STRIKING A BALANCE

The creation and development of shared interests help to solidify some couples. As each partner invests energy into a mutual project, he or she entrusts part of himself or herself to the mate. This reciprocity strengthens the bonds of cooperation and joint enterprise. Each partner feels a greater commitment to making the marriage work and has more to lose by splitting up. An effort is made to keep the relationship ongoing and stable. This frequently requires holding back disappointments, hurt, and anger "for the good of the family." The ensuing loss of spontaneity is overshadowed by the gratification gained from the sense of unity.

TRYING TO RECAPTURE ROMANTIC LOVE

When spontaneous loving impulses do occur, they often evoke feelings of closeness which reawaken the desire to relate romantically. However, the previous loving intimacy is difficult to recapture. By now each partner has been hurt many times in trying to fulfill his or her fantasy of love. Each has learned to seek protection from this pain by suppressing those feelings which menace the relationship. To maintain the positive connection, the pair must put themselves in a bind. While holding on to the model of intimacy which originally brought them together, they must check the spontaneity which made this oneness possible. When a couple is actively engaged in the pursuit of a joint goal, however, the bind and frustration become more tolerable. Besides their solidarity, they have their pride in accomplishment as compensation. There are couples who can maintain this balance indefinitely by Hanging In with shared interests. They accept the limited closeness and lack of intimacy while feeling secure that the bonds between them will sustain togetherness. Resentments and loneliness are rarely, if ever voiced. For other couples, the suppression of feelings is more, troublesome; the thought of maintaining a relationship without passion and intimacy is unacceptable.

In the Hanging In stage of becoming a couple the passion is displaced onto external tasks. This sublimation has many secondary rewards. Having children, gaining possessions, accumulating wealth, and obtaining credentials, generally bring praise and approval from family and friends. The fulcrum of motivation shifts from pleasing one's spouse to gaining recognition from others. This trend diminishes the symbiotic aspects of the early marital unity while increasing those traits necessary for effective social interaction.

Thus far, both partners related through their fantasies, became disenchanted when these constructs were not fully realized, unsuccessfully tried to change each other, and became angry and hurt over the loss of their early love. In the power struggle to recapture the fantasy neither submission nor domination worked. The pair are faced with breaking up the marriage or finding a suitable substitute for their previous intimacy. They must do this conjointly or, again, suffer the strains of a torn relationship. A balance has to be struck between family and environment.

CHILDHOOD TRAINING
FOR HANGING IN

Stabilizing the marriage through the incorporation of external gains is a process requiring considerable skill and tenacity. Spouses must learn to work cooperatively without getting too emotionally involved with each other. Their past history together makes it unlikely that they can sustain such closeness. If they do become too emotionally involved, they are unlikely to pursue their external goals. On the other hand, if they become overzealous in their tasks, they jeopardize their marriage. When a baby, home, or promotion becomes more important than our mate's reaction to this accretion, distancing inevitably follows. The delicate balance necessary for the success of this period of marital development largely depends on the couple's strength of commitment to their relationship while engaging in mutually agreed upon goals. Fortunately, the years spent in our parent–child relationship provide most of us with training for this family–environment duality.

After the child exhausts himself or herself (and oftentimes, the parents) in an unsuccessful bid to realize omnipotence, he or she is ready for school. Here, the child can sublimate the need to master the family by becoming proficient in reading, writing, and arithmetic. When parent and child consolidate their relationship through a mutual interest in school, the rewards are many. Besides the youngster's mastery of the subject matter, his or her pride is associated with being loved at home. As the ego expands, the child can pursue curiosity into other ventures. The child feels secure in reaching out to the world, since he or she is emotionally taking along the parents. Sharing these discoveries and experiences can be a source of family unity and pleasure. Parents, too, flush with satisfaction as they see their youngsters accomplish those tasks that are meaningful to them. Helping a child with homework and reading him or her a story can be highly rewarding to such parents. Even though the tenderness and intimacy of babyhood are gone, both parent and child can relate warmly through this shared interest.

By the time children enter school, the symbiotic tie to their mothering one is greatly reduced. Rather than seek a return to their earlier status as baby, they cannot wait to engage in "grown up" activities. While some of this impetus is a reaction to lingering wishes to return to the breast, their physical, mental, emotional, and social development dictate the need for self-fulfillment elsewhere. However, they have neither the skills nor self-confidence to face these challenges on their own. Support and encouragement from home are necessary for success. Helping children to "let go" of their dependency and to channel the bubbling energy into outside activities becomes a new role for parents.

The secure and confident adult welcomes this opportunity to loosen these dependent bonds. Besides freeing time, the easing of responsibility helps to encourage this parental shift. However, mixed with pride and esteem for this hallmark in their child's development, the parent feels concern for the youngster's well-being. It is no more easy for a mother and father to accept abruptly their offspring as independent than it is for the child to feel confident. Monitoring the child's social activities helps some parents allay their anxieties. Time, and a host of positive reinforcements, is required before both parent and child can redefine the youngster as self-sufficient. The duration of this hanging-in period varies with each set of circumstances. Poverty, parents' illness, other children, as well as increased family responsibilities may hasten a child's ability to care for himself or herself. The sequence and period of the youngster's development, along with parental attitudes toward this change, will largely determine the outcome of such growth. If participation in outside activities establishes family unity, the child is likely to evolve an individual identity at maturation. Such a background helps prepare the youngster to hang in successfully when he or she arrives at the corresponding stage in becoming a couple.

The attitude of parents toward their offspring's accomplishments is important. If they are indifferent to the child's undertaking, the child most likely will not be motivated to do well. If they are not interested in his or her education, the youngster feels disconnected from home while having to deal with a strange environment. This often gives rise to behavior problems in school. For instance, one way a child can involve parents is by being sent to the principal's office for disobedience. The child can also sit in class passively while fantasizing all kinds of exciting events. When the teacher calls home to express concern, the parents are likely to take notice. In these, and other ways, it is possible to re-ally with the lost family. The success of this strategem, however, largely depends on the parents' ability to be responsive to the basic problem.

Parents can also be overly anxious that their child do well in school. If a good report card is more important than the youngster's satisfaction in learning, the parent–child relationship will suffer. Children are quick to perceive that they are subordinate to their parents' concern for external success. They can, amongst other things, rebel and do poorly or become phobic about leaving home. The power struggle is reshaped by whose interests predominate. Maintaining the emotional tie to the mothering one is fundamental to the child. Expressing this closeness by living up to the family value system is more important to parents concerned with external success. The power struggle takes them back (or is an extension) to the "fearsome fours," where the parent–child relationship is defined in negative terms. Developing skills to deal effectively with the environment under these circumstances is highly unlikely.

Overprotective parents are another source of difficulty in the child's maturational process. Perceiving the youngster as too weak and unprepared to meet the challenges of school and neighborhood alone, they unduly intervene in any activities away from home. The child remains emotionally tied to parents at the expense of self-confidence. Since parents cannot indefinitely insulate their young from life's exigencies, such "protection" is self-defeating. Sooner or later the child must make a decision alone and face the consequences of that judgment.

Children of such parents grow up feeling inadequate and dependent, thereby increasing the likelihood of making poor choices in their social interactions. This leads to the circularity of making them more reliant on parental control and intervention.

Frequently, the motivation of overprotective parents is less than benevolent. Feeling unfulfilled in their own marriages, being uncertain of their ability to deal with the establishment, or having little sense of importance except as a parent, may lead such individuals to use the child to act out their own conflicts. The resultant dependency is likely to cause the youngster to remain close to home, echoing the decisions of mother and father. Another dependent response is for the child to defy such solicitude by behaving contrary to the expressed parental stance. Such youngsters are not developing a sense of self, inasmuch as their definitions are in reaction to those upon whom they depend. Defiance is not independence.

INCORPORATING SOCIAL VALUES

It is during this period of acculturation that children incorporate society's values. Here, gender differences are strongly inculcated in both sexes. Organized games, group singing, and school rituals lay the groundwork for cooperative behavior. Making friends and visiting their homes help broaden a child's capacity for understanding and effective self-expression in society. When the family's value system is consistent with the child's behavior, the developmental sequence of the parent–child relationship goes smoothly. If the youngster is out of step with the family views, or they with the youngster's conduct, a clash is unavoidable. How parent and child reconcile these differences will form the foundation for compromises in adulthood. The style of these interactions will remain the format for future arbitration.

Parental attitudes toward achievement in school, sports, friendship, and other social activities is basic to this stage of the child's growth. Five-year-old children do not have the option to leave home. They have to hang in. If their needs go unfulfilled or clash with their family, they will either withdraw, seek satisfactions elsewhere, or revert to a power struggle to alter this condition. If all struggles prove fruitless, the child's self-image suffers while dependency increases. In such a case, outside relationships are likely to prove unsatisfying. Such children grow up emotionally insecure and easily influenced. If they follow the path of withdrawal, they are likely to have inordinately active fantasy lives. Living effectively in reality becomes difficult for them. Being in touch with personal needs, finding adequate outlets to express them, and successfully interacting with the environment while remaining emotionally attached to the family is a complex process for any child. Those children who are helpless and dependent in their family life and fail to achieve satisfaction outside the home have a difficult time in growing up. The sequence of their development is a shaky progression from symbiosis to independence. Such unstable arrangements in the parent–child relationship are poor preparation for Hanging In when they face similar circumstances in their marriage.

Adults from such backgrounds have little experience to encourage their Hanging In during this phase of becoming a couple. Most instances of shared activity with family members have been painful. No matter how well-meaning their intentions, maintaining a loving kinship while goal oriented is very difficult for them. Often, the marital relationship is relegated to a lowly position while accomplishment is held supreme. This, of course, strains the marriage. Some individuals give up trying to relate to either their spouse or the outside activity. They withdraw and become morose. This condition is unstable, usually forcing their mate to become more decisive and authoritarian. It is during this period of marriage that people with poor Hanging In preparation in their original families tend to develop obesity, alcoholism, drug abuse, uncontrolled gambling, and a host of other self-destructive conditions. It is also a time when psychologically related physical illnesses surface. These reactions heighten dependency. At first, such symptoms usually generate concern and care. This is short lived, as spouses become despairing and resentful of their mate's helplessness. They become angry and pull away. If they do not find some meaningful excitement away from home, they, too, will become depressed. Many individuals in this condition, however, feel too insecure and frightened to terminate the marriage. Despite their misery, they feel stuck. Feeling incapable of achieving closeness to their mates, obtaining gratification elsewhere, or leaving, they suffer in their hopelessness.

Wendy, for example, found it increasingly intolerable to hang in, in her marriage. She felt stuck. If she expressed disappointment and resentment, David would withdraw. If nothing changed, she was fearful of pursuing her feelings for other men. Sharing her concerns with David might jeopardize the relationship. The thought of divorce panicked her. She considered having another baby as one possibility of Hanging In. Her previous experience, however, taught her that infant care would be too confining. She was thus stuck with her own dependence. Feeling this way meant that self-assertion was too hazardous. She could either wait and hope for David to mellow or find the courage to take risks. If she could overcome the impediment of her dependency, there might be a way out of her entrapment.

Several options are open to Wendy. One possibility to lessen her dependent position would be "doing her own thing" in areas that minimally threaten her relationship. She might continue her graduate education or find a job that takes her out from under David's wing. Part of Wendy's dilemma in such a choice, however, is the fear of losing her dependent position. If she does not *have* to stay in the marriage, Wendy is not certain she would *want* to hang in. She cannot know what she wants unless she experiences herself as having a choice. To feel free to choose, she must renounce being directed by others.

Feeling stuck in a dependent position is not solely a woman's problem. Many men, who relate to their wives by taking care of them, are also helpless to change their marital style. It is easier for men to be oblivious to their dependence, since they generally have more opportunities to assert themselves outside the home. They can hang in, in their marriage for long periods without focusing on the lack of gratification in their relationship. When their dissatisfaction can no longer be ignored, or if their wives behave in a fashion that endangers the marriage, they become painfully aware of their own dependence and fear of separation.

David has made it clear that Wendy's interest in other men is a crucial issue for him. If she challenges him in this area, he will be forced to recognize his reliance on her. It is possible, in the interest of maintaining an active involvement with Wendy, that he will redefine his priorities. For instance, he might socialize more. It is also possible for him to discover his own emotionality and the freedom to express it. As long as Wendy tolerates this stalemate, however, David is unlikely to move. His fear of accepting his own dependency prevents him from initiating such a step.

DEALING WITH
DEPENDENCY NEEDS

How members of a marriage deal with their dependency needs is central to the Hanging In stage of becoming a couple. The gradual increase in self-confidence, trust in one's mate, and display of mutual concern make the acceptance of such traits possible. It is the quality of experiences and confrontations in marriage that, in the long run, tells the story. The longer a couple hang in together, the greater the chances for this accommodation. Shared experiences, both agonizing and joyful, afford each partner an opportunity to display empathy toward his or her mate. The more such events accumulate, the more interdependent they become and the greater the difficulty in separating. At times, the choice is seen as a life or death issue.

A woman who wanted to leave her marriage after twenty-five years said, "If I stay, I know I'll die." Her husband responded, "If you leave, I'll die." At that moment both were more fully alive than they had been for years.

The goal of marriage is to remain happily connected. Most people associate feeling connected with feelings of love. The illusion, in the loving condition, is that the connection occurs by being loved. This is a common misconception. Rather, it comes from the misuse of the expression, "I love you." What is almost always meant is, "I love the self that I am when in your presence." It is the active *I* doing the loving that generates this exalted state. It comes from within ourselves; it is not a condition bestowed upon us by someone else. The presence of a particular other may bring this loving connection about most intensely or frequently, but it is not the other who "does it." Our readiness to emotionally release ourselves to this person is the chief ingredient of love. However, the only other relationship that comes close to this subjective feeling is that with our early mothering one. Through this association we attribute the power to feel loving to our marital partner. Herein lies the problem: It makes us dependent on this person.

In the developmental progression of becoming a couple, this dependent condition must be dealt with effectively. We must duplicate, more or less, the maturational process of the child; that is, we must proceed from symbiosis to independence. The gradual relinquishment of the marital fantasy generally follows the course of increasing self-assertion. This is expressed through our efforts to recapture our early romantic love. Because we still believe the power of love comes from our partner, self-assertion takes the form of attempting to force this result. During the Honeymoon Is Over phase, when we felt disenchanted, we tried harder to please our mate in order to get this power released. When that did not work, we tried, in the Getting Even phase, to influence our partner to submit to our wishes. Still looking to our significant other for loving feelings, we invested our passion in the struggle for power. The presumed prize of winning such a quarrel was the control over our spouse to elicit loving behavior. But how can anyone be made to act lovingly? We may succeed in controlling others by threat and guilt. But forcing them to love us—never! The word *love* comes from the Latin "liber," meaning free or liberally expressed. Love is, then, the freely expressed concern, desire for, and wish to please another. It cannot be forced out for our convenience.

THE FAILURE OF CONTROLLING BEHAVIOR

The controlled behavior resulting from power struggles is rarely satisfying to either spouse. The consequence is generally two people who are angry and hurt. When the anger and hurt accumulate enough to threaten the relationship, the couple generally turn to external tasks as a means of holding their marriage together. In this sequence the issue of dependency is typically ignored. Placing the emphasis on effective behavior helps to bypass the problem. This reaction to the helplessness of feeling deprived has many gratifications. Thus, the Hanging In stage affords the couple a sublimated outlet for their desire for intimacy while protecting them from the discomfort of facing their dependent needs.

By acquiring a baby, a business, an advanced degree, or a house, two people can express their love for each other indirectly. They redirect their energy toward being effective in outside endeavors. Neither is trying to control the other. Neither has to worry about being dependent, for both are externally focused. While the passion of the relationship is primarily invested in an area of mutual concern, a couple can feel positively connected. The dependency problem has not been resolved; it has been temporarily set aside.

Depending on the areas of mutual concern, Hanging In can last from one year to an indefinite period. If one project does not bring happiness, the process is not questioned; instead, another outlet is found. At some point in this phase of marriage some people, still feeling disappointed and deprived, will turn to individual pursuits instead of seeking gratification with their mate. One couple spent three years building a house. When the last project was completed, and the husband still did not feel the passion he had been missing, he became interested in another woman. While building, he focused more on how he would feel when finished than on how he felt at the moment. He never seriously questioned his lack of intimacy. His experience was that the house was done and "all of a sudden," he found himself in love with another woman. Those who have been more actively involved in striving to fulfill themselves in their relationship are more apt to recognize and acknowledge their disappointment and deprivation. Pursuing gratification on their own represents a conscious choice emanating from their direct experience with their mate. Ultimately, this is less destructive to the relationship. Doing Your Own Thing, in this manner, offers the potential of developing sufficient self-confidence and skills to confront the marriage honestly.

5
chapter

DOING YOUR OWN THING

How specific couples evolve from the unity of The Loving Relationship to the individuation of Doing Your Own Thing is quite varied. The length of time they remain in any one phase, the degree of overlap between stages, and the impact of each area on the total relationship, all influence the development of the marriage. In some instances, several phases exist concurrently; that is, Getting Even, Hanging In, and Doing Your Own Thing interactions may be going on at the same time. In addition, each spouse is not necessarily in the same place at the same time. A husband can be involved in Doing Your Own Thing while his wife is invested in Getting Even, or vice versa. One of the pair may be Hanging In while the other alternates between Getting Even and Doing Your Own Thing. The combination of a husband engaging in Doing Your Own Thing while his wife is Hanging In with small children can be fairly stable and gratifying. This may evolve, subsequently, into the wife engaging in Doing Your Own Thing while the husband is Hanging In with older children. Regardless of which variety and style of interaction a couple follow, they must deal with their respective dependency on one another for the fulfillment or absence of their love needs. Dealing with this issue may be anywhere on a continuum of daily confrontations on the topic to absolute silence. At some point, most couples confront each other with what they are missing and what they want to change in the marriage. For approximately forty percent of marrieds, this encounter takes the form of divorce.

JOHN AND LUCILLE:
A CASE IN POINT

Lucille and John have been married fifteen years and have two children, twelve and ten years old. John works as an accountant, expending a great deal of energy "making it." Financially, at least, he is successful. He functions with a good deal of pressure, which he frequently relieves by drinking. On these occasions he is often nasty to his wife and children. At first, Lucille was frightened and confused. She felt intimidated and helpless to change the situation. This evolved into hurt and resentment toward John's behavior and attitude. As the years went on, she became increasingly alienated.

Two years ago, Lucille decided to take some college courses. She thought her feelings of emptiness and desperation would be relieved by studying English literature. She did well the first semester and signed up for two more courses the following term. She became friendly with one of her instructors and before the second semester was over, had been in bed with him several times. This was the first time she had been sexually involved with someone other than John. She knew she was not in love with her instructor, nor he with her. She also no longer felt in love with her husband. Her education, both formal and personal, had led to her feeling more confident and less frightened and helpless. She felt a greater sense of her own value. The next time John came home semi-intoxicated and nasty, Lucille told him she wanted a divorce. Despite her husband's protestations, the following morning she consulted an attorney.

John was devastated by Lucille's action. He pleaded with her to give him another chance. He promised he would stop drinking, become a better father, husband, and person. Lucille was adamant. She had been very hurt by his treatment of her and the children. Most crushing of all, she no longer loved him. John was beside himself. They had several huge quarrels, with Lucille insistent on leaving and John alternately contrite and threatening.

This was the first time they fought overtly. Up to this point, Lucille's position was that of silent, suffering victim. She had not only repressed anger but never displayed any strong emotion. As for John, he never did take full responsibility for his hostility, blaming it, instead, on the booze. As painful as the fighting was, it was refreshing for them to be expressive of their deeper feelings. Now, interspersed with their anger, they were making passionate love. Encouraged by Lucille's excitement, John took her to see a gorgeous new house. He told her it was expensive but they could afford it if they stayed together. Lucille softened her stance and agreed. They decided on Hanging In and decorating their new home.

Before very long John went back to drinking and losing his temper. Lucille was infuriated. She ordered him out of the house and called the police. John did not know what hit him. Before he knew it, he was living alone, had a restraining order barring his return, and was utterly confused and depressed. He could not even have a satisfactory telephone conversation with Lucille. She was in no mood for talk and vague promises. Either he was going to seek help or they were finished. John agreed to go into psychotherapy and to try to control his undesirable behavior.

Returning home, John became painfully aware of his dependence on Lucille. This was the chief topic in his therapy. He could not fathom the rapid turn of events. Most of all, he was surprised at how lost he felt without his family. His construct of home had placed *him* in the most responsible and powerful role. Relating equally as well as intimately was an unknown experience. He could not firmly grasp what was really wrong. He learned to control his drinking—but that did not help. He became more attentive and considerate. Still, Lucille remained cool and aloof. She, in the meantime, had returned to school for further study. She was having a blast exploring new relationships. While not indifferent to John, she would challenge the least sign of his taking her for granted. She vowed never again to return to her silent, suffering role.

In due time, John and Lucille became involved in struggling for power. He got his second wind and, impressed with his own self-discipline to stop drinking, became more involved in raising the children, furnishing the home, and even in suggesting Lucille's manner of dress. Each of these areas had become grist for the power struggle mill. Lucille enjoyed John's new-found interests but no longer accepted as gospel his view on how life should be lived. Her new self-image reflected confidence, self-assuredness, and independence. Occasionally, she came to John's therapy sessions to air her understanding of him and the status of their marriage.

EARLY EXPERIENCES

Lucille, the younger of two siblings, was raised by an alcoholic mother. During Lucille's formative years her mother would have inexplicable rages, verbally and physically abusing her children. When the liquor wore off, she was depressed and, sometimes, apologetic. Lucille tried to cope with this periodic chaos by being careful, unobtrusive, and "good." Feeling loved by her father and accepting his direction to "not aggravate Mother," she learned to stay out of the way when her mother was drinking. She tried hard to please and behaved as if everything would be all right as long as she remained quiet. She was married at nineteen, going from her parents' home to becoming John's wife. Lucille never seriously addressed herself to the question of who she was and never considered what she was going to do with her own life, other than to complete the familiar picture of wife and mother.

John was the middle of three children. His father was a policeman-stern, authoritarian, and rigid. His mother was frightened, passive, and compliant. She expressed love to her children by fulfilling their physical and material needs. The family life was detached and empty. John learned to express his emotional needs through personal contacts outside the home and through achievement in school. He was competitive, albeit not very confident, and his accomplishments were gained at the cost of considerable pressure and anxiety. The approval for his successes that he sought from his father was never forthcoming. He gave up attempting to relate to either parent and concentrated, instead, on getting awards in school. When he met Lucille, John welcomed the opportunity to be effective in caring for such a needy and responsive person. Being six years older than Lucille, he never questioned his wisdom to know better than she what was best for their relationship. Despite this seeming confidence, he was still seeking approval after fifteen years of marriage.

John and Lucille have, thus far, miraculously escaped divorce as a solution to their unbalanced relationship. Both had terribly poor backgrounds in preparation for marriage. Their respective fantasies of a loving relationship are worlds apart. Despite this unlikely combination, they remain married. Both are quite bright, very stubborn, and highly devoted to their respective attachments. She, to her notion of a happy family whose members have discrete roles; and he, to his investments—one of which is family.

Lucille's life with John paralleled the relationship to her mother. She accommodated and placated both, being too frightened and dependent to do otherwise. A good deal of her hurt and anger toward John belonged to her mother. The intensity of these feelings so terrified her that rather than express them, she ceased showing any emotion at all. However, this state could not be sustained. Lucille's innate vitality and power sought an outlet. When she was engaged in Doing Your Own Thing, excitement reemerged. She could no longer contain her pent-up emotions. Nevertheless, since expressing hostility directly was not her style, she chose to separate. John's dependent reaction made Lucille feel more powerful and secure. This combination of feelings lessened both her helplessness and her dependency, leading to her altered family role. This change enabled Lucille to remain true to her basic nature while staying attached.

John, like his mother, saw providing money and material objects as love. He assumed Lucille would be fully satisfied by his economic productivity. He further pictured her as responding with loving feelings to gratify him. Lucille, on the other hand, fantasized John as totally self-sufficient, requiring nothing from her except motherhood to complete his happiness. She believed he needed no rewards other than success in business and a a healthy family. To Lucille, initially, John was the knight on a white horse. Her romantic images of love did not include a needy, self-doubting husband. As long as John maintained his essential role as breadwinner, Lucille could sustain Hanging In because the marriage invested her with the identity of mother. When John's belief that he could cope with business pressures without confiding his need proved incorrect, the marital balance was irreversibly upset.

REACHING OUT

During the Hanging In stage of marital development the couple's passion is sublimated through some external activity. When this external source fails to provide the sought-after love, partners have increasing difficulty believing that such happiness will come from their mate. Once a spouse begins to doubt gratification will come from his or her counterpart, that spouse must decide to live without it or seek individual fulfillment. Living without love is a painful existence. It is an especially lonely condition. If an individual is too frightened or dependent to pursue personal happiness, he or she may have no alternative but to live without love. Although some people live out their lives in this fashion, in our judgment this is an untenable condition, requiring progressively greater self-destructive behavior to avoid the pain of such isolation. Most individuals will, somehow, find the strength to reach out to some facet of the environment in order to make a meaningful attachment. When this occurs successfully, there is often a personality change. Some personal quality is found enabling the renunciation of that previous role which led to the static position. A new role is taken. Through reinforcement this change may become a permanent part of the individual's repertoire of relating. If it can be integrated into the marriage and sustained, it will lead to a basic change in the dyad. The couple will either separate or alter their marital style. *Doing Your Own Thing is that process of reaching out to the environment, relating to others, seeking emotional gratification previously associated with the marital partner.*

When a member of a coupling is in the Doing Your Own Thing stage, he or she begins to question the partner's ability to gratify his or her dependency needs. Occasionally, along with questioning the partner, the spouse engages in analysing the dependent self. Some part of the self that had been lying dormant may be reawakened in the process. Typically, when this happens, a flood of energy is released. This fuel becomes an available resource in the marriage. The matrimonial state may have been so weakened by deprivation that remaining attached is in jeopardy. A spouse who brings fresh energy into such a marriage at this juncture may, indeed, be saving it from destruction. When Lucille tells John she is no longer interested in playing out their old marital scripts, she is stopping and reversing a deadening process in their relationship. Individuation almost always loosens the binds that tie a marriage together. When these binds are injurious to the needs of one or both participants, a way must be found to alter this destructive condition while maintaining the marital attachment. Doing Your Own Thing affords the couple such an opportunity.

When Lucille married at nineteen, she was doing her own thing in relation to her family. Once she married, her primary involvement shifted from parents to John. Vis-à-vis her parents, doing her own thing was a separation. It is not surprising, then, that Lucille's pursuing her own interests led to a separation from John. Many people, especially those who enter marriage as a means of leaving home, are afraid to individuate from their mate because they perceive it as a forerunner of separation and divorce. For Lucille, doing her own thing, while relating to John, is exploring new territory and is, consequently, a big step toward growing up.

As difficult as it is for some individuals to succeed on their own and take responsibility for their lives, it is even more difficult to grow up and be their own person in a relationship. To be self-sufficient and responsible *for yourself and the relationship* is perhaps the greatest challenge of all. While Lucille decided to seek her own fulfillment, she was doing so in reaction to John's irresponsible parent and husband behavior. By proving to herself that she could obtain pleasure away from home and, to John, that she did not need him, she discovered personal resources hitherto unknown. This self-assertion directed a lot of energy into what had become a stale relationship. It forced John to realize his own dependency needs and pushed him into exploring this issue. When Lucille ordered John out of the house, the relationship was fundamentally changed. She was not only responding to her new-found freedom but to her perception that John, and the way he related to the family, needed to be transformed. Doing Your Own Thing enabled Lucille to muster the courage and skill to make this repair. Luckily, Lucille, like most of us, had an opportunity to preview this stage during her childhood.

A CHILDHOOD PREVIEW

Once children feel confident that they can interact with the environment and still be connected to home, they are ready to discover those people and interests particularly suited to them. Their increased perception, confidence, and skill enable them to relate in areas disassociated from family. Close friendships, belonging to exclusive clubs, and engaging in distinctive activities hold high priority for these youngsters. Childhood is a time when special names, codes, and secret arrangements predominate. There is great pride in feeling positively unique and "special," particularly when such feelings transcend the family circle. For children between the ages of eight and twelve, a secret shared with a close friend can be more important than any event at home. The emphasis is on self-expression, independent of parental supervision. Disdain is shown for dependency on adults, as well as for an inability to run with the crowd. These preadolescents are determined to acquire peer values and acceptance. That this is a displacement of dependency from parents to peer group is never questioned. The gang's appraisal becomes more important than parental praise. These youngsters are no longer following the prescribed family course of action. They are doing their own thing.

As long as such conduct does not lead to trouble or disrupt family routine, parents, generally, do not interfere. Although mothers and fathers may be interested in their offspring's activities, they are rarely willing to actually participate in such experiences. Playing hopscotch or Johnny-on-the-pony, pretending to be a "Trekkie" from outer space, and using secret code names is not typical adult behavior. Just as preteenagers know they do not belong in their parents' card game, bowling night, or private talks, so, too, parents intuit when to stay out of their child's involvements. These are mutually exclusive activities that enhance the functioning of each family member while not threatening the relationship. Like work, school, or marketing, they are acceptable temporary separations. Beyond being tolerated, these activities are often encouraged. Not only does greater independence occur through self-expressive behavior but evidence mounts that both parent and child bring the excitement generated outside the family into the fold. This helps make individuation and, ultimately, emancipation more palatable in the parent–child evolution. It further helps prepare for the acceptance of Doing Your Own Thing in marriage.

Some parents find it difficult stay out of their child's play. They are overanxious that something will go wrong, have very strong values that are important to imprint on their young, or use this involvement as substitute fulfillment for empty marriages. In any case, the need for individuation is frustrated and the dependency tie prolonged. Such interference complicates the youngster's personal growth and encourages undue attachment to the home. Likewise, children who constantly stay around the house or follow parents to their recreational events tend to sustain their emotional reliance on the family. Having adequate outlets for self-expression beyond the family is necessary for mutual respect in the parent–child relationship.

When parents display neither interest nor concern in their preteenagers' activities, their youngsters may become anxious. They may feel rejected, unwanted, unloved. To play with friends is pleasurable, but not when you have to worry that such behavior leaves you completely detached from home. Children want both the excitement of play away from family and a sense of parental approval for such independent activity. Indifference, or nonrecognition of this circumstance, does not help the child effectively deal with his or her dependency needs. The child cannot do his or her own thing and at the same time feel proud about growing up in accordance with the parents' values. The child will regress to a dependent state at home, get into difficulty outside, or develop an emotionally unfulfilling set of relationships. He or she will be poorly prepared for the corresponding sequence in marriage.

Eight-year-old Craig, for example, had just begun to do his own thing by acquiring a best friend. Craig had become much more self-sufficient, riding his bicycle around the corner to visit his friend and occasionally sleeping at his house. He was also asserting himself a great deal more in school, sometimes causing the teacher to discipline him. This took place at a time when Craig's mother returned to work full time. Being preoccupied with her own readjustment to the work force, she was oblivious to Craig's independent behavior. Within two weeks, Craig began to display symptoms of fear and regression. He cried at night to his mother, "I don't want to go to school—I'm scared." Mother and child were instantaneously reunited. Craig stopped seeing his friend and returned to a helpless, dependent role. His mother, concerned and guilt ridden, reduced her working hours to correspond to her son's attendance at school.

Couples coming from such backgrounds do not have a smooth experience during this phase of their marriage. They interpret Doing Your Own Thing as a threat to the dyad. Sometimes this threat is limited to their partner's activity; oftentimes, to the actions of both. For some couples individuation on the part of one partner is tantamount to divorce. The "All for one, one for all" motto of such pairs is really a cover-up to keep them dependently tied. Were this dictum true, then "All" would accept the "one" during individuation. Again, the problem is in recognizing and accepting the mutually reliant aspect of coupling. The denial and/or rejection of this bind leaves the pair helpless to propel their relationship along progressively mature paths.

Lucille, for example, was initially helpless to cope with her dependency on both her mother and John. Not until she entered Doing Your Own Thing and realized that an alternate life style was available could she face her previous condition and overcome it. In the course of this maturation she also recognized, for the first time, John's dependency on her. While *he* was shattered upon seeing his true state, Lucille kept right on pushing him—into therapy, into stopping drinking, into taking greater responsibility—until he gained sufficient strength to be her equal. Lucille knew only too well the horrors of being helplessly stuck in a dependent role. Her commitment to family enabled her to employ her insights and power to remedy John's condition so that they could be more equitably matched.

Some women in Lucille's circumstance would be too angry and vengeful to repair the marriage. Upon gaining strength, they would attack and undermine their husband and then leave. No longer needing to hold the relationship together the old way, they would not seek to establish a new basis for relating. Although such behavior is understandable, it limits the consolidation of important personal gains and undermines the subsequent use of this strength in a new relationship. For many women, getting a job, going back to school, or having an affair can generate and release enough self-confidence to overcome a dependent marital role. However, this may create a vacuum in the marriage. Something has been removed from the coupling, while nothing has replaced it. Unless a replacement is found, divorce is likely. Men, too, change their jobs or have an affair that opens their eyes to their own value and importance. Those who leave the marriage, rather than apply their insights to remedying the situation, lose an important opportunity. In our practice of couples psychotherapy, all too often second and even third-time-around marriages present a replication of dependency symptoms. Those partners who do not attempt to use their new-found independence to help an ailing marriage tend to repeat their crises in subsequent unions.

MAINTAINING THE CONNECTION

While Doing Your Own Thing is part of a progression from the symbiotic love tie to individuation, it does not necessarily follow that the implementation of this step will lead to independence. In the development of a couple, Doing Your Own Thing is generally a reaction to the loss of dependence on a marital partner. Having lost the belief that love and happiness will be forthcoming from this spouse, the deprived mate seeks gratification alone. This does not mean that this deprived mate wants to end the marriage or even to continue being self-sufficient. What is happening is the gradual recognition that his or her depiction of the spouse is incorrect; that the person with whom he or she is living is different from the idealized image of a loved one. Nor does it necessarily follow that this increased independence will be used to improve the quality of the marriage. Since more realistically viewing the other, the deprived mate may accept that, indeed, they are different, requiring their own unique outlets for fulfillment. Although still attached, they have diverse interests. The chief significance of this stage is that the dependency of at least one partner is greatly reduced. This, of necessity, shifts the balance in the marital scale. To maintain a vital connection under these circumstances, some new arrangement must be found. Most couples who get this far in their development opt for a modified sharing of their respective individualities.

The most common examples of modified sharing are the weekly card game, tennis match, or fire department meeting. These are unilateral social activities having an emotional significance previously associated with the marital partner. The pair have ceased confronting each other on their respective deprivations; instead, they now sublimate through others while maintaining a stable but unpassionate attachment to each other. Such couples tend to deal with their separation fear during this marital phase through a peripheral involvement in each other's activities. That is, the card game may have a kitty used for the players to socialize once a year, or the players may take turns playing in each other's houses. The fire department may have an annual dance; the tennis partner could be invited to a party. By occasionally meeting their mate's companions, spouses overcome the sense of being left out of that involvement. In this fashion a husband and wife can maintain strong emotional ties outside the marriage without threatening the primacy of the marital relationship.

By such interactions, couples can sustain their relationship without having to deal with their misgivings and doubts about the nature of their marriage. They can still maintain their fantasies of love and the prospect of each returning to the basic symbiotic roles. The focus remains on the illusion that the partner possesses sufficient power to bring about the early loving connection. This basic belief, the foundation of their love, is difficult to renounce. However, after Doing Your Own Thing, it becomes increasingly cumbersome to sustain this view. Sooner or later, the couple will confront each other with what the marriage lacks. It is often expressed as, "There should be more sex," "I don't feel as passionate as I used to," or "We hardly do anything together anymore." At this juncture in the marriage, each partner is less dependent and more self-confident. Thus, there is a greater likelihood of the marital dissatisfactions being voiced constructively. Yet the prospect of a confrontation is frightening. Some couples tend to hedge. Others stall for time. All would like a reawakening of passion and a safe outlet for its expression.

This is the time of the "Seven-year itch." The unexpressed ardor is transferred onto someone found to be sexually exciting. Often, this person is a younger version of the displaced mate. In this relationship, the marital disenchantment is acted out. Rather than accept disappointment and seek solutions within the marriage, these partners attempt to reaffirm their faith in the fantasy. Their passion shifts to experiencing a warmed-over version of The Loving Relationship—only with someone other than their mate. As long as the time-and space-limited aspect of this relationship is intact, such an outlet can, like The Loving Relationship phase, last up to two and a half years. Inevitably, however, this coupling must either progress to a full-range relationship or terminate. If it becomes a substitute love affair, it may lead to a divorce from the original partner and a replaying of the marriage scene. Sooner or later the reliance on fantasy for excitement must be faced—if not with this new spouse, then with the third! Passion, ultimately, must find an outlet in reality.

Sometimes this passion is expressed through a sequence of Getting Even, Hanging In, Doing Your Own Thing, Getting Even, Hanging In, Doing Your Own Thing. The confidence gained in Doing Your Own Thing is mixed with a fear of separation. This combination of emotions is then expressed in the form, "If only *you* would have done as I asked you *to*, I wouldn't *have* to go out and do it myself, thereby risking a separation." The satisfaction gained in Doing Your Own Thing becomes diluted by seeking blame for the marital emptiness. The more fundamental issue for such spouses is their fear of detaching from each other. They do not have the faith, commitment, or skills to trust that pursuing their own emotions will strengthen their union. For many couples this is true. Couples who spend many years Hanging In—raising children, for example—suddenly find themselves confronted with a stranger when their youngsters leave. Having little to say to each other, they have to force an interest where there is only mild curiosity. Doing Your Own Thing, at this point, can be a real threat to the relationship. The couple may need some time, afforded through the circularity of the preceding sequence, in order to be able to deal adequately with each other.

In addition to time, the pair searching for a close unity, rather than attack each other, must learn to trust that expressions of deprivation are designed to clarify personal exposure. To achieve this understanding, however, each partner must use his or her sensitivity to the other to remain positively attached while voicing dissatisfactions in the marriage. This can be tricky. Keeping a balance between honest self-expression and protecting the feelings of your partner is often quite delicate. This may have to be done many times, in a variety of ways, before each member of the dyad can truly hear the other.

NO FAULT DEPRIVATION

One of the reasons such communication is difficult is that it hinges on the acceptance of a no-fault concept of deprivation. In order to accept that one or both spouses can be deprived without the other's malevolence or ineptitude, the notion of a partner's power to fulfill the fantasy must be challenged. One must be prepared to relinquish, or at least modify, the picture of a harmoniously fulfilling loving relationship. Not many couples are eager to do this. Ultimately, the issue is decided by the relative strengths of the individual's need for fantasy fulfillment and the marital connection. If the personal need is greater, acceptance of no-fault deprivation is unlikely. If the relationship is fundamental, renunciation of the fantasy is possible. Doing Your Own Thing can help distinguish between fantasy needs and reality fulfillment and bring increased objectivity to this decision. However, the situation, at this crossroad, is complex and influenced by many variables.

At least three factors are developing concurrently. First each partner is becoming more self-sufficient and less reliant on the other. Along with this development, each spouse has an increased awareness of what he or she wants out of life and in what ways the marriage is deficient. Second, compared to outside activities, the marriage has become less exciting and meaningful to both partners. Third, the transactions between the two have become more complex and interwoven. Besides the shared interests and time together, each spouse has struggled with his or her mate in dealing with respective fantasies, deprivations, and hurts more than with any other person. These highly charged investments have, over the years, made the relationship profound and diverse. The two partners are truly related. While this tie makes it easier for the spouses to articulate their dissatisfactions, each partner's declared limitations to provide these needs become more credible. At first, there is disbelief at the expressed helplessness of each partner. (It is still difficult for each to believe that the other does not have the power to bring love and happiness.) This suspicion, generally, is rationalized, interpreted, distorted, and forgotten many times over before it begins to sink into each spouse that they are, in fact, telling the truth; namely, that they are helpless to make each other happy. For some couples the confidence and sincerity of each mate finally helps the message get through. If they have enough courage to acknowledge the reality of their own experience, one and/or both will recognize the hopelessness of their quest. At this point they will be ready for the next phase of becoming a couple, namely, Giving Up.

6
chapter

GIVING UP

Sheila and Bob are a handsome pair married twenty years. Wherever they go, they are admired individually and as a couple. They are bright, fun-loving, and adventurous. They are highly articulate, expressing strong views on most aspects of living. Publicly, they appear united and happy. They are a formidable team when their logic and passion blend. Yet alone, they fight constantly. There is hardly a subject upon which they agree. It does not take much provocation to set them off. Their lives are full of turbulence and controversy.

Besides two teenagers from their union, they each have grown children from previous marrages. Some earthshattering issue is always taking place in their household. Despite their manifest alliance, their solutions generally differ. These issues give rise to a volatile relationship, characterized by years of their struggling to change each other. Thus far, there is a stand-off, with each stubbornly maintaining an individual outlook. As neither can get his or her own way, each obtains satisfaction by periodically punishing the other. Bob frightens

Sheila with his rages, while she gets even through alcohol and drugs. They appear to take great delight in torturing each other. They hurt enormously yet vow never to experience the pain and disruption of another divorce.

Frequently they spend days brooding and sulking. Whenever either has had enough solitude, "instant contact" is achieved by each confronting and challenging the other. Closeness also occurs through their attention to outside calamities. Just when they seem to reach a crescendo of destructiveness, a crisis arises involving family, work, or neighborhood. Instantly, the couple unite to meet the threat. They defend their familial status with the same vigor employed in their arguments. Usually, they remain physically and emotionally close for several days after each catastrophe. During such periods they respect and adore each other immensely, recapturing their sexual ardor. Throughout the two decades of their union, both Sheila and Bob sustained the belief that if they could be free from parental responsibilities, they would achieve a perpetual state of honeymooning.

Recently, a mutual urge to recapture the passion that initially brought them together led them to try a church-related encounter weekend. As a result of this experience they were closer than they had been in years. They were able to sustain this intimacy for several weeks. Their lustful connection terminated, however, when Bob had trouble with his oldest son. Sheila disapproved of her husband's handling of the situation and, as usual, pulled no punches in speaking her mind. Bob was unprepared for his wife's criticism. He felt terribly crushed—betrayed. Moments earlier they had been lovingly united. How could she assail him so cruelly? Bob erupted with a vicious attack, physically hurting Sheila. She recoiled in rage. Finally, with deliberate self-control, she said, "Damn, if I can't speak my mind freely to my husband, then I can't anywhere. You can take your closeness and shove it. I give up." She expressed the helplessness and despair for them both. Each knew they were not going to separate or look for another relationship.

They settled back into Doing Your Own Thing, cooling their involvement. Yet this distancing was different. Through their tears they expressed sadness over their lost romance. This time they somehow knew it was no one's fault. Bob treated his son according to his own value system. Sheila was authentic in communicating her views. In their closeness, each assumed that they were in the same place. Each believed that the unity was so complete that whatever one felt, so did the other. They were not prepared for the reality of their divergence. Their nervous systems could not take the abrupt and complete separateness. It hurt too much.

Despite their disappointment, communication continued. They discussed their inability to sustain their romantic love. They could even joke about their circumstance. They spoke of running away from home together. They knew that would not work. They considered separating and meeting clandestinely. They could not afford that. They thought of alternately spending six months apart and six months together. They could not live with such an arrangement. They looked at their situation from every angle—and agreed to give up. Giving Up meant no longer expecting to sustain a passionate loving connection. It was like mourning a parent. The only consolation was in their sharing this loss.

During this period Sheila had a vivid dream. She dreamt she had lost her wedding ring. She panicked in her sleep, until she looked at her hands and realized with relief that the wedding ring she had lost was from her right hand, not her left. When she wondered about the meaning of her dream, Sheila realized that what she had lost was some fantasy and illusion about herself. She also knew that despite her hurt and disappointment, she was committed to continuing her marriage. What she was giving up were her fantasies of how the marriage *could* be, as well as her expectations of how it *should* be.

EARLY EXPERIENCES:
SHEILA AND BOB

Giving Up is a condition that both Sheila and Bob experienced in one form or another since childhood. Their respective backgrounds inexorably led to the surrender of their idealized concepts of marital unity. Neither could have planned such a process of becoming a couple.

Sheila was raised in a materially comfortable Catholic home, the oldest of three children. Her father was an attorney who expressed contempt for many people he considered beneath him, including his wife. Sheila's mother was afraid of her husband's sharp tongue and, after the birth of her third child, began to drink to take the edge off her constant tension. She related to Sheila by being critical when sober and helpless when drunk. Sheila responded by assuming increasing responsibility for the house and her younger siblings. She related to her mother by trying to please and protect her. She emulated her father's articulateness, often verbally sparring with him over one of his favorite scapegoats. This combination led her to grow up looking confident and competent, a model daughter and student. However, her confidence was more apparent than real. She was vulnerable to criticism and expended a great deal of energy trying to be what she thought others wanted.

Sheila went directly from her parents' home to her first marriage. She related to her husband in the same dependent manner. Early in this union her husband started to drink and was sexually unfaithful. When Sheila learned about his infidelity, she divorced him. There was little in her background that enabled her to enter into the give and take of trying to work things out. She was incapable of confronting her husband with her anger and disappointment, opting instead to separate permanently. It was well into her second marriage that, unable to confront her husband and unwilling to separate herself emotionally or physically, *she* resorted to drinking. In this fashion she could carry on the power struggle while still maintaining her dependence. It was a way of coping she had originally learned from her mother.

Bob was an only child. His father was an engineer and his mother a school teacher. As an infant and youngster, Bob was doted on and played with by both his parents. He was the center of their lives until he was three and a half years old. At that time, a severe economic strain led to his mother's abrupt return to work. Bob was placed in a nursery school, where his advanced speech and keen mind brought much positive attention. However, the emotional climate at home was relatively sterile. He learned to contain his feelings in that serious and worried household. He was undemanding and isolated from his parents and, later on, from his peers. He grew up denying feelings of helplessness and need, acquiring self-esteem through his ability to accomplish tasks.

As a young adult, Bob found sexual activity an important area of emotional expressiveness. In the course of a sexual involvement he fell in love with his first wife. The sexual attachment did not mean as much to her as it did to him. After they were married, she looked to him for other kinds of emotional responsiveness. When it was not forthcoming, she became increasingly unhappy and, ultimately, could not respond to him in the one area in which he was available. They drifted apart, remaining involved only in their mutual responsibility for their children. After his wife fell in love with another man, the marriage was terminated. When Bob met Sheila, the mutuality of their sexual passion enabled him to fall in love again. This time the feeling was reciprocal, with Sheila's initiating sex as well as responding sexually. Sheila's verbal expressions of passion during love-making led Bob to a new level of emotional expressiveness which continued throughout their relationship.

Both Sheila and Bob had developed strong fantasies of intimacy as a reaction to their marital failures. They had each tasted closeness in their first marriages and experienced a prolonged and painful struggle with their loneliness before and after divorce. When the symbiotic unity of their second mar-

riage began to fall apart, they found themselves in an increasingly painful bind with no apparent solution. They would not
split. They could not renounce their idea of how marriage
should be. Yet every attempt to recapture their earlier intimacy
led to more hurt. Sheila's bouts with alcoholism were a direct
reflection of this bind. It became increasingly clear that if she
continued to go in that direction, she would be giving up her
life. A decision to live meant staying sober, entailing more involvement with herself than with Bob. This led Sheila into
Doing Your Own Thing via Alcoholics Anonymous and a job.
As she pursued these activities, she put emotional distance
between herself and her husband. It was, therefore, most painful to reinvolve herself in the marriage encounter experience
only to be followed by the intense quarrel and subsequent
dream. The ensuing depression was most remarkable in that it
did not lead to a return to alcoholism—a condition on which
Sheila was literally weaned. Instead, she chose to relinquish
her imagined picture of happiness. She somehow garnered the
strength and courage to remain attached to Bob without any
hope of their relationship improving.

ACCEPTING THE REALITY

While the loss of fantasy and illusion is accompanied by sadness and depression (it represents, among other things, relinquishing one's childhood), it can also lead to a more gratifying
marriage. The loss is felt by both partners, even if only one is
going through the process. If the wife gives up her illusions,
the husband is powerless to reinstate them or ease the accompanying depression. If he is emotionally attached to her, he will
feel and share her loss and sadness. Such an interaction can be
bittersweet, poignant, tender, and close. If the husband does
not become defensive (back to Getting Even) or try to fight the
lost illusion with another five-year plan (back to Hanging In), a
different involvement is possible. The ultimate acceptance of
the reality that marriage cannot sustain those childhood images

of love occurs during the Giving Up phase of becoming a couple.

What is given up is (1) the idea that one can live happily ever after; (2) the hope of changing one's spouse to achieve such happiness; (3) the hope of changing oneself to achieve such happiness; (4) the sense of omnipotence that one can create and sustain a relationship of one's choosing; and (5) the attempt to live in the past, with its righteous recriminations, or in the future, with its expectations.

At some point, we all must accept our helplessness and vulnerability. We either learn to recognize and experience available gratification or continue to be periodically disappointed. In marriage, it is easier to blame our deprivations on our mate, thereby clinging to our illusions as long as possible. Indeed, the need to retain such fantasies can be so strong that some couples will divorce rather than give them up.

FACING THE CHALLENGE

What enables some pairs to go through the Giving Up phase of marriage after five years while others never achieve this stage? Out of our experience with hundreds of couples, we, the authors, have isolated three conditions that seem to accompany a couple's ability to face this challenge. These conditions are the couple's total commitment to achieve intimacy, both partners' ability to tolerate and function while under great stress and pain, and a background of personal deprivation and sacrifice for the unity of family.

Both Sheila and Bob, after their respective divorces, felt keenly their separateness. Having tasted intimacy with their first mates, they were determined to reexperience this condition. However, both wanted such closeness to be total. Besides the fulfillment of a sexual union, they wanted freedom to express themselves emotionally in the presence of their mate. They wished to be open and spontaneous, desired to share most of their interests, and, above all, needed to trust that their mate would stand by while they went through whatever phases or conditions were necessary in order to be ready for such a close relationship. In each case, a deep, soulful yearning for intimacy can be traced back to early childhood, where a warm symbiosis was aborted too soon.

Each member of the dyad also has a long history of functioning under stress and pain. Sheila's loss of her nurturing mother to alcohol and her subsequent responsibility for the household and care of her siblings was more than adequate preparation for this state. Her divorce and vow never to reexperience such a marital break further led to her ability to function with much pain. Bob, too, learned early in life to live with tension and pain. The abrupt loss of devoted parents to economic privation, as well as the shift from a rewarding nursery school to a tense household, helped build his tolerance for strain. When his first wife withdrew her sexual involvement, Bob felt deeply the pain of his isolation. He remained faithful until she terminated the marriage.

Both Sheila and Bob are strong family-oriented individuals. Each comes from a background where family unity is accompanied by much sacrifice and deprivation. Sheila's father constantly spoke of remaining married "for the good of the children," even while berating his wife. Her mother all but destroyed herself rather than leave the union. Sheila lost her childhood to responsibility quite early in life. Despite her bleak marriage, she remained devoted until her husband had an affair. Bob, likewise, learned of self-sacrifice for family unity. Both his parents worked hard to maintain a household deemed proper for him. He checked his natural spontaneity to maintain the family mood when he returned from school. He devoted himself to achievement, despite his yearning for a return to the nurturing days of his early childhood. Both partners possessed the motivation, character, and ability to tolerate adversity to help reach the Giving Up stage of marriage.

Paradoxically, the same sense of determination and ability to function alone when striving to fulfill idealized goals are necessary in the Giving Up phase. To remain attached to one's mate while relinquishing all illusion requires a strong ego. Having enough energy available for this shift in focus also contributes to a successful coupling process. A good deal of energy is attached to fantasies and expectations. When these are given up, the energy is available for living in the present. One can become more fully involved in each here-and-now experience. Very young children live totally in the present. As they mature, the socialization process trains them to anticipate the future. Giving up immediate gratification for future rewards is a crucial aspect of learning. Although the focus of energy changes at different stages of life, some balance must always be maintained between living in the present and living in the future.

The problem with anticipating the future is that it must be done in fantasy. When the future arrives, it has to be experienced through our expectations. One person's euphoria over getting a raise, for example, can be another's disappointment. It depends on what was expected. With couples, each transaction is filtered through their expectations. In most instances, these are different. How a couple accommodate to this difference determines the style of their marriage. If the goal is to maintain the attachment, despite disappointments, the couple will remain anchored in the present. There is less focus on expectations as each tries to clarify a position. Attention shifts from disappointments to how to understand each other. If the goal, however, is to fulfill one's wishes, then the quality of the interaction suffers. Except for The Loving Relationship and the early symbiotic connection between parent and child, having both the fantasy and the connection is virtually impossible. However, by struggling to achieve this combination, the futility of realizing an idealized closeness becomes apparent. Where there is no struggle, the fantasies and illusions remain unquestioned.

The process of Giving Up goes on, however, whether or not it is overtly recognized. Sometimes it is played out through a couple's children. When a youngster does not act according to parental expectations, an attempt is made to get him or her to comply. When this fails, the parents may be allied by their misery and disappointment, experiencing solidarity in relinquishing their aspirations. If the hopes for fulfillment persist, one or both parents may blame the other or the child. Some attachment is then going to deteriorate. In those households where parents struggle to get close, the children are likely to do the same. A dialogue takes place where respective positions are aired until everyone becomes reasonably clear in perceiving the others. In such homes the fantasy of an idealized connection is given up in order to maintain close relationships. If the illusions are not renounced, real ties are not possible. Energy has to shift from an investment in the idealized relationship to actually relating to the real people at home. This holds true even if the nature of the relationship is sharing the loss of the fantasy.

Giving Up is an active stage in a relationship. It is different from the fixed distance of Hanging In. Nor is it the same as the parallel functioning of couples who stay together indefinitely in Doing Your Own Thing. It is meant to describe those couples who are at a point in their relationship where *they* are more important to *each other* than the ideas they brought to the union. They may share the sadness of losing those constructs. They may nostalgically mourn their lost loving relationship and know they can never again experience such innocent love. This stage is an acceptance of each other "as is" and a commitment to remain attached regardless of circumstances. It is a vow to the person you are living with, rather than to your idea of that person. It is entrusting oneself to another. For some, it is also a faith that they will find a way to remain married no matter what events take place.

GIVING UP IN ADOLESCENCE

This stage of couple formation has its counterpart in early adolescence. When a child of thirteen has been doing his or her own thing for a while, he or she becomes aware of the conditional nature of parental love. As a result of independence the child begins to formulate a sense of who he or she is. In the beginning of such a construct, the child tends to be clearest about who he or she is not. Gradually, through trial and error, a self-image that generally holds up in a variety of circumstances evolves. As the youngster's confidence increases, the self-image becomes firmer. At some point the youngster will realize that parental wishes clash with his or her own. Wanting to relate by obtaining parental approval, the youngster tries to train them to accept his or her self-image. The adolescent still depends on their love but wants them to relinquish their standards to comply with his or her own. This inevitably fails. Then the youngster may openly rebel, challenging the family to accept a divergent life style. They rarely can. The next few years are spent testing how independent the adolescent can be and still remain attached to the family. As he or she trades off personal desires for parental approval, the youngster gradually realizes that their acceptance is less and less important.

While giving up the need for parental approval, the adolescent loses the sense of idealization of family. No longer expecting to live in harmony with the parents, the adolescent knows he or she cannot change them and has the confidence to successfully withstand their attempts to alter his or her behavior.

The foregoing process takes place through confrontation and struggle and is accompanied by pain and anxiety. It is not a smooth transition. It is important that youngsters have some parental standard to which they can relate and/or rebel against. Parents who are too indulgent or undefined make it more difficult for their youngsters to know themselves. As with couples, there is a separation process for parents and children that enables adolescents eventually to give up their dependent position and come to some definition of self. There are teenagers, however, who cannot emotionally separate from their parents without actually leaving home. These are the adolescents who will have a more difficult time dealing with their dependence when they are in a couple relationship.

In our culture most teenagers do not separate from their parents. In their attempts at individuating, they tend to remain at home, where they often revert to a Getting Even or Doing Your Own Thing interaction. When they do depart, it is usually to get married. At times, their choice of a marital partner is a reflection of either a power struggle or a rebellion against parents. But this indirectness lacks the benefits of an overt confrontation. It is likely that they will be stuck in a similar position with their mate. It may take a divorce, as with Bob or Sheila, before they are ready to commit themselves to working out a relationship regardless of the pain and anxiety that this entails.

REEXPERIENCING OMNIPOTENCE

For some children, late adolescence brings with it a resurgence of omnipotence previously experienced in the Oedipal stage of relating to parents. These teenagers are clearly committed to living out their childhood fantasies, rather than giving them up. Reality will eventually catch up with them, either in coming to terms with their marriage partner or with their own children. Sooner or later, if they choose to be in a real relationship with a real person, they will have to give up their illusions and fantasies.

Giving Up is accompanied by feelings of loss and depression. The feeling of mourning is real, as the loss is real. When the fantasy of the connection is gone, one experiences more separateness in the actual relationship. Boundaries are less merged. One has a greater sense of where one ends and where one's mate begins. One is also more aware of one's aloneness, intensifying the sadness. Giving Up is not linear in direction: In the sadness and loss there are many attempts to reestablish the old fantasy. Both partners cooperate in this. The fantasy cannot be sustained, however, and if there is no pretense, the process of Giving Up eventually reasserts itself and again becomes overt.

Giving Up is now added to the ongoing cycle of Getting

Even, Hanging In, and Doing Your Own Thing. It takes many times around before the finality of the loss is realized and before the couple is ready to accept each other's personality. All illusions are gone. Each partner acknowledges a role in creating the unobtainable connection. Each knows that the marriage cannot be any different than the involvement of the two real partners and that this would be true of any dyad that either might form. Now a renewed interest takes place in each partner's personality. The depression lifts as avenues for an exploration of the relationship begin to emerge.

7
chapter

GROWING UP

Growing up is the acceptance of what is. Fantasies are relegated to nostalgic memories. In their stead comes a rediscovery of the beauty and complexity of life. To grow up is to renounce the expectation of being fulfilled by others. Autonomy and self-reliance become proud accomplishments that prove more sustaining than dependency or symbiosis. Yet there is an inherent need to relate to others. How to maintain one's integrity while interacting becomes the principal skill of this phase of marital development. The Growing Up stage is a new beginning; it is a partnership of mutual interest in the rediscovery of each other. It is living in the present—the taking of one's pleasures now. Facing the limitations of being human helps to savor each morsel of the here-and-now experience of intimate connections. The passion of The Loving Relationship is replaced by the glow of close friendship and loving concern for each other.

In The Loving Relationship, the couple's energy is expressed through the fantasy of the symbiosis. In The Honeymoon Is Over phase, the emotional intensity is directed to trying to please each other in hopes of recapturing the previous loving connection. Getting Even finds the couple using their power to manipulate and punish each other for not providing the desired love. The excitement of the pair is displaced onto children, career, house, or other involvement in the Hanging In stage of becoming a couple. The intensity of Doing Your Own Thing focuses on self-fulfillment through external accomplishments. Giving Up finds the energy turned inward in the struggle to overcome the habitual desire for the early symbiotic union. Growing Up allows the energy to flow spontaneously outward, enabling a direct experience of the marital interaction.

The long trek from the symbiotic tie of The Loving Relationship to the self-sufficiency of Growing Up tests many times over the "glue" that holds a couple together. Fortunately, the chemistry that attracts partners to each other is inherently reciprocal. What one finds desirable in a mate is a quality one values and requires for oneself in order to feel complete. For a variety of reasons, one cannot integrate this trait as one's own. (Men, for example, often find it difficult to accept their tenderness, while women have trouble with assertiveness.) This attraction makes each partner dependent on the other. During the early stages of marriage the fulfillment of these dependency needs helps to strengthen the coupling as each partner gains maturity. Ultimately, both must own up to their respective needs and find the courage to provide them for themselves. But then they no longer need each other for the expression of these traits. What tends to occur is a gradual build-up of mutual respect and acceptance, so that each partner becomes a source of support and encouragement to help the other master such skills. They are friends cheering each other on to new and more challenging modes of self-expression. Each takes pride in the mate's accomplishments, without having too much at stake in the outcome.

Similarly, the *manner* in which a couple typically interact is also reciprocal. A man who has learned to relate to others by attending to their wants will feel a sense of familiarity and belonging to a woman who has developed a style of relating through her needs. On another level, the man needs to be needed and the woman accommodates by being needy. Each is acting out a script from childhood, connecting via the way they learned to relate to their mothering one as they progressed from infancy through childhood to adulthood.

In the Growing Up phase of becoming a couple, the reciprocal attachment begins to dissolve. When one gives up fantasies and illusions, the rationale for replaying the old script disappears. When such behavior continues, it is from habit. There is not enough energy to sustain this unrewarding mode of relating. Gradually, it atrophies. In addition, as each member of the dyad matures, he or she no longer ascribes to the mate the power to gratify. The man who needs to be needed, for example, begins to recognize that the needy woman he married never developed the skills to care for him his way. He accepts this condition as a reality of life—no longer to be struggled against. He can now chuckle at the absurd wish to have a needy person take care of one who is need-fulfilling. As he expressed his need, she became *needier*. Clearly, this reciprocal arrangement has built-in limitations. In Growing Up, this restriction is finally acknowledged and accepted.

A couple entering the Growing Up stage of marriage are often puzzled by the observation that they are capable of a wider range of self-expression outside the marital relationship. The needy wife, for instance, is quite adequate in gratifying others, taking on her husband's role. He, in turn, finds it easier to be receptive to care from people other than his wife. This paradox may become a source of mutual interest and exploration. Each can view the other with renewed wonder, trying to figure out how this seemingly impossible feat is managed. New respect is generated as they observe each other's adequacy with others. This reciprocal appreciation usually is accompanied by greater self-acceptance of one's own capacities as well as limitations. A rediscovery of self slightly precedes, and runs in tandem with, the detection of changes in one's mate. It is necessary to know and accept the reality of oneself before one can know and accept the reality of one's partner. This is what characterizes the Growing Up phase of becoming a couple.

BEGINNING TO GROW UP: MARILYN AND GLENN

Marilyn and Glenn have been married twenty-six years. Their three children are young adults who fluctuate between independence and destitution—physically, emotionally, and financially. After their youngest child went off to college, they found themselves alone for the first time in over two decades. They had been going through a difficult time and approached their new "freedom" with apprehension. They had settled into a careful attachment, aware of their missing excitement and afraid that prolonged togetherness would underscore their estrangement. In part, their loss of passion was due to the cessation of struggle and a concomitant vow to accept the relationship "as is." Although the decision to give up the struggle was not overtly stated, it followed a mutual desire to end the pain and frustration of the past few years. They had also stopped talking about their relationship, as that, too, evoked the hurt and disappointment of realizing the distance between them. In short, they had given up and were now afraid to face what each experienced as the emptiness between them.

Marilyn, the oldest of three children, was raised in a Jewish family heavily oriented toward religion and children. Marilyn's maternal grandmother died a month before she was born, marking her arrival with both great joy and sadness. For two and a half years she was completely overprotected. Her mother was everywhere, watching the baby as though she were a fragile princess. Fortunately, a sister was born when Marilyn was almost three. The intensity of her mother's attachment was abruptly diluted. Although the new involvement was less binding, the earlier relationship remained indelibly etched into her personality. Whenever Marilyn wished to be joined with her mother, the quickest way was for her to be needy. While her mother was preoccupied with the second baby, Marilyn began to grow into a bright, capable child. She enjoyed expressing her competence away from her parents. As a young woman, Marilyn continued this duality. She was competent and effective away from home; dependent and somewhat helpless within her family. When she met Glenn, she was attracted to his intensity, worldliness, and desire to please her. Her mother's lack of enthusiasm for her boyfriend made him more, rather than less, attractive to Marilyn. When they were married, she moved from her parents' home into Glenn's apartment.

Glenn, the second of four children, was raised in a home where the key word was survival. His family was on Home Relief during the depression. By the time Glenn was eight years old, he had a thriving shoeshine business, as well as approval from his mother for the money he brought home. Glenn's mother had a deprived childhood and was chronically depressed. She nursed her first son through his constant illnesses, welcoming Glenn's self-sufficiency. By the time he was ten, Glenn understood, and was resigned to the fact, that there was no way he could make his mother happy. He shifted his attention to his father and was able to feel much more competent and effective in taking care of him. When he was fourteen, Glenn went into business with his father. He provided the money to get them started and made most of the financial decisions. By the time he met Marilyn, Glenn was in college preparing to become a dentist. For him, she had just the right combination of competence and need, self-reliance and vulnerability.

At first, it seemed they were made for each other. She worked while he went to school. Away from him, she was capable, confident, and effective. With him, she was dependent, somewhat helpless, and seeking his approval. Despite her good sense, she generally deferred to his judgment. He went into private practice and shortly thereafter their first baby was born. All Marilyn's time was devoted to being a wife and mother. She became more dependent and less confident, while Glenn became more assertive and expansive. In his office he had daily feedback as to his effectiveness. In their home she was constantly reminded of her ineptness.

As the family grew, so did the demands on both of them. Glenn thrived on his ability to make money. Marilyn foundered on the shores of motherhood. She had been able to maintain some balance in her relationships as long as she had an identity outside the home. When she relinquished this role, the balance fell apart. She perceived Glenn as watchful and critical of her behavior and decisions. She tried several different ways to get out from under his wing, but nothing worked. When their youngest child started kindergarten, Marilyn returned to school. She now embarked on doing her own thing.

As she became more comfortable with her outside identity, Marilyn exerted more authority at home. She began to struggle with Glenn (as she never did with her mother), challenging his dominant role. Glenn was unaccustomed to having his power questioned. He felt misunderstood and unappreciated. As the struggle became more intense, he began to withdraw. He initiated a series of affairs, carefully selecting partners with whom he would not get seriously involved. The one quality all his lovers possessed was their commitment to gratify him. Marilyn, in the meantime, increased her investment in her budding professional career. The distance between them grew. She completed training as a social worker and threw herself into her work. Once she felt secure in her professional life, she tried pursuing Glenn. When he was unresponsive, she shifted to an indirect involvement through their children or some project of mutual interest. At one point, feeling angry, rejected, and deprived, she threatened to leave him. For a while, he was attentive to her and they were a little closer. However, their closeness was frustrating. Their old brand of relating was no longer satisfying and new styles felt unstable.

They traveled the circle of Hanging In, Doing Your Own Thing, and Giving Up many times. When one of them pulled away, the other found some new venture to keep them going. They bought and fixed a beach house, developed some farm property, and started a new business. They were successful in all their enterprises, achieving sporadic intimacy. However, they could not break out of their old mold. Sooner or later, no matter how they started to reunite, Glenn's dominance and Marilyn's need surfaced as their predominant style of relating. Finally, they both gave up and settled into a friendly distance. They snuggled in bed but had little sex. Both openly acknowledged their commitment to the marriage despite the lack of gratification. They were nostalgic about the past and happiest when they shared a positive milestone with one of their children. At this point, their youngest child left home.

Slowly and tentatively, they began to reach out to each other in new ways. Marilyn invited Glenn to an interactional workshop she previously would have attended alone. Glenn enjoyed his wife's involvement and shared in her excitement. Even more important, he allowed himself to be vulnerable in what was, for him, unfamiliar territory. In turn, he invited her to go fishing, something he normally did with his friends. They began to mingle joyous parts of their lives that heretofore were separate. In doing so, their manner of relating changed. She became more innovative and adventurous. He basked in the warmth of her vitality. She was sexually assertive. He let himself be "done to." They were like adolescents discovering each other. This time around, however, they had the inner resources to sustain this new unity. They were more realistic and pragmatic in reaching out and responding to each other.

Vestiges of their old relationship still were present. While enjoying each other, they were most susceptible to the disappointment of unexpected separations. If one turned to others, the partner felt twinges of jealousy and hurt. Preoccupations, misunderstandings, and loss of interest on the part of one could cause anguish in the other. Many instances of happiness followed by disaffection were required before the couple could master their newly found togetherness. Luckily, the pressure to reattach in the old way was not great. In addition, they each had fully established activities and interests outside the union that constantly reassured and supported them. When ego insults arose within the marriage, they were balanced with an abundance of external positive feedback. Also, both Glenn and Marilyn were aware of the temporal nature of life. Besides their parents, many of their friends had died and the threat of terminal illness hung like gossamer all around them. This helped keep them in the present and searching for ways to accent the positive. Finally, they repeated Katherine Hepburn's adage, "The ability to forget helps keep you young." Letting go of past hurts was essential in making room for new pleasures. Awkwardly, they thus continue to explore new modes of interaction.

Marilyn and Glenn are at the beginning of the Growing Up stage of becoming a couple. As in any new relationship, their joyous reunion will gradually be replaced by expectations. What is different for them is that they have another model to follow and the confidence that stalemated marriages can be changed. Both have been able to relate to others in a present-centered, no-expectation manner and know what to do when they want to bridge the distance between themselves. They have learned to live with the persistent pull toward their symbiotic tie. Under stress or when threatened, the tendency to revert is ever present. This has become part of the reality they recognize and accept as necessary for mature living.

THE DIFFICULTIES
OF SEPARATING

In most societies marriage is the primary interpersonal relationship for the majority of adults. Although other associations exist, they are ordinarily goal-directed, time-and-space-limited arrangements. Sex is generally a central feature of marriage.

Along with this personal physical exposure, an emotional release typically occurs as the union is consummated. This emotional state—this spasm of surrender—in the presence of a mate is the closest experience to complete fulfillment that most people have since infancy, when they were cuddled and fed by their mothering one. This physical, emotional, and deeply trusting oneness is the principal haven of retreat most people define as home. Together with their partners, individuals evolve characteristic roles to ensure the continuation of this state. When they succeed, a couple begins to form—a process that takes years and a select progression to complete.

In the beginning, marriage is a place to act out years of anticipation and fantasy without fear of censure. Here, as no where else, each member of a couple can expose his or her uncertainties, shortcomings, and limitations while still feeling acceptable. The arrangement allows a deep sense of security and belonging but tends to fixate the marital roles. There is a trade-off of commitment versus personal growth. To expand or reverse their roles would bring the partners into conflict with the fundamental worry of all intimate relationships, namely, the Big Fear.

This basic human concern—separation and the dread of being alone—prevents more couples from facing reality and growing up than any other single factor. People can feel miserable, stuck in an unhappy marriage, on a treadmill of Giving Up, and still not move toward Growing Up. The pain and fear associated with a separation are so deeply ingrained that all manner of horrors are tolerated within a marriage rather than chance a break-up. Sometimes the fear of facing a split is imposed by the death of a mate or a divorce instituted by one's partner. Such forced separations help some individuals experience the dreaded pain and loneliness, thereby enabling them to go on to accepting the reality of depending on themselves for gratification. Besides the need to separate in order to experience the expanded aspects of one's personality, courage, resourcefulness, skill, and perseverance are required. With few exceptions, couples need the understanding and support of each other to enable this step to be taken within the marital relationship.

EXCHANGING MARITAL ROLES

In the Growing Up phase of becoming a couple both partners start to take on for themselves those qualities they found attractive in the other. As she pursued her career, Marilyn began to feel and express the power and authority characteristic of her husband. When she gave vent to this state with Glenn, the marriage shifted. Whereas previously the relationship had revolved around Glenn's position, Marilyn's new-found attitude began to play a more dominant role. Because the connection was reciprocal, Glenn had to be ready to relinquish some of his egocentricity. Similarly, as Glenn accepted his own vulnerability, allowing his dependency to surface, Marilyn had to be willing to fulfill his needs. The balance in the marriage continued with the participants exchanging roles. Both felt more complete in this new arrangement as they became freer to express those parts of their personalities previously hidden. It was no accident that this reversal took place, since these traits were part of the initial attraction between them.

Separating from the symbiosis is not necessarily the same as keeping oneself separate. Besides the reversal of roles described (a cleavage in the symbiotic tie between Marilyn and Glenn), any attachment not associated with one's earliest bind to the mothering one is potentially available for a revised union. The need to separate, for purposes of individuating, is only temporary. Separation, here, is used to mean emotional, rather than physical, apartness. This partition is necessary because of the influence exerted on all subsequent intimacies by the dependency of the early parent–child relationship. To overcome this influence, a diversion from the source of dependency fulfillment is helpful. This enables an individual to draw from private resources that which was formerly obtained from another. Again, the chief obstacle is the Big Fear.

The dread of loneliness can be seen in the difficulty couples have in separating. In Growing Up, separation takes place through the struggle within marriage: One has to fight with one's mate for the privilege of feeling separate from this person. Since there is a reciprocal bind in marriage, it takes two to let go as well as to connect. Having defined themselves in terms of their marriage, partners are not likely to surrender their statuses without some contest. Sometimes the rejected partner will vindictively withdraw all support previously taken for granted. Frequently, with the reaction of "I'll show you," the rejected mate leaves the rejecting one. Helplessness, depression, illness, and all the symptoms of the Getting Even stage may resurface at this time. These tactics can be of sufficient force to postpone or even prevent Growing Up from getting off the ground. However, if a person is willing to struggle hard enough for individuality within marriage, Growing Up can proceed despite these obstacles. It may follow the bumpy road of a constant encounter, but the accomplishment is ultimately appreciated by both members of the union.

This encounter can be precipitated by the loss of a parent or a child. Marilyn, for example, returned to college when her youngest child started kindergarten. Both she and Glenn entered the Growing Up phase of coupling after this youngster left home. The departure of family members helps to bring out our essential separateness. Although the absence of a loved one tends to generate memories and fantasies of reunion, it also drives home the temporal nature of our existence. In such an atmosphere, turning to oneself for completeness in the here and now often occurs. But when this loss finds one living with a mate, the pressure is to come to terms with this reality conjointly. If there exists a wide discrepancy between partners mourning the loss of a loved one, the separateness is felt more keenly. If the loss is experienced about the same, the couple may be motivated to seek more vital ways to relate and act out the need to find pleasures together. In either case, the departure of a loved one can set off the process of Growing Up.

When one achieves emotional autonomy, perceptions of loved ones change. For instance, as parents, the focus shifts from how children see you to how you see them. You become more firmly anchored in your own being, viewing the world from that perspective. Similarly, there is a recognition of children's rights to live their own lives and make their own mistakes. Their behavior is seen less as a reflection on you, the parent, than as a comment on their own struggle to mature. This altered view tends to influence the typical style of interaction of such family members. Usually, greater self-respect and confidence accompanies a genuine appreciation for the loved ones' individualities. Less energy goes into trying to change them and more into enjoying them for what they are. The sense of responsibility shifts from them to self. No longer believing their behavior is a reflection on you, you can more fully enjoy yourself in their presence. That is why so many grandparents and grandchildren are delightfully close.

Growing Up does not automatically follow Giving Up. Illusions and fantasies can be given up, as well as expectations of one's mate, and an individual can still be locked into a symbiotic embrace. On the other hand, Growing Up *cannot* be accomplished unless Giving Up has taken place. It is the giving up of illusions and fantasies that enables one to live in the present. In Growing Up, one not only lives in the present but accepts responsibility for gratification, for difficulties—for one's life. Feeling autonomous and in charge of one's self frees the energy formerly locked into expectations and the struggle to recapture the symbiosis. There follows an availability to be connected to one's partner, and the world, in a much more intense and all encompassing way. A 79-year-"young" woman said, "In order to feel alive it is important to be attached to something—even a plant; to watch it change and grow."

THE TRANSITION FROM
DEPENDENCY TO SELF-SUFFICIENCY

As Growing Up within a marriage requires the cooperation and support of both partners, the successful maturational process involves a harmonious interplay between parent and young adult. Parental approval and encouragement generally accompany a youngster during his or her years spent in preparation for autonomy. Where the developmental progression has been smooth, and parent and child have been in agreement, the transition from dependency to self-sufficiency is usually without incident. People with such a background have the greatest likelihood of achieving Growing Up in their coupling. For a large proportion of the population, however, there are countless obstacles to overcome before this stage can be reached.

As our society becomes more technologically advanced, the years of preparation necessary for productive employment increase. Throughout this length of time youngsters remain dependent. It is no longer rare to see people in their late 20s or early 30s still receiving financial and emotional support from their families. This makes it difficult for an individual to embark upon a course of action contrary to parental wishes. Besides the fear of separation, concern over the loss of support tends to keep most young adults compliant with their family's values. When these standards conflict with an individual's needs, the individual must modify either the parents' rules or his or her wants, or both. If the young adult is to remain emotionally attached to family, he or she must, in addition, do this conjointly with the parents. Since most parents tend to govern their children with that yardstick which worked best for themselves, a congenial alliance is not very likely. A frequent way out of this impasse is for the youngster to leave home. Where the departure is in harmony with the family's outlook, such as college or working for a friend or relative in a distant city, confrontation is avoided and the struggle put off to a later date. Sometimes, an early marriage is used to escape the conflict between parent and child. Postponing the struggle affords the young adult time to develop more confidence and the skills to become self-reliant while the parents accommodate to the loss of their offspring.

The transition from home to college can be very challenging for some teenagers. A year on their own, having to "make it" in an unfamiliar environment, being responsible for governing themselves, making decisions that materially affect their lives, and, in some cases, supporting themselves can help speed the maturational process. Besides the absence of parental care, facing the practicalities of daily living for the first time can be quite an education. Assumptions and beliefs about the world's attitude toward them can turn naive adolescents into seasoned cynics. As life experiences help to define them, these youngsters can develop clearer distinctions between themselves and those they depend upon. As self-reliance increases, so does the ability to judge and accept oneself. Greater independence also increases one's capacity to accept others for what they are. For those adolescents who can use going off to school as an opportunity to grow up, one of the rewards is an expanded view of their parents. They see them more as the kind of people they are and less as "just" parents.

Not everyone can separate emotionally by leaving home. Some children maintain a fantasy connection when away from their parents. Although they are ostensibly on their own, they monitor everything they do as though their parents were actually on the scene. When they return home, they quickly fall back into the familiar dependent state. In an important sense they have not separated. One young woman left home to become a "ski bum"; that is, she worked at a ski resort for the privilege of spending all her spare time skiing. When she had been there six months, her parents took a ski vacation at her resort. The first day they were on the slopes together, she skied into a tree. While she was being stitched and bandaged in the emergency room, she realized that all the time she had been on her own she was watching herself as though she were literally her own mother. Once her mother came on the scene, she apparently stopped watching herself.

Physically leaving home is not the same as emotionally coming to terms with one's dependency. Marilyn, for example, left her parents to become subordinate to Glenn. Glenn, in turn, reenacted his early family scene by establishing a similar relationship to Marilyn while away at college. Nowadays, young people travel a great deal, physically distancing themselves from their early nest. However, the task of growing up is more complex and requires a greater involvement than taking a plane ride to Europe. The first goal of psychological maturation is becoming aware of those sets of beliefs and concepts which sustain dependent behavior. Once having isolated these constructs, it becomes necessary to develop independent ways of caring for oneself. All this has to be accomplished with a partner who participates in the struggle. Unless such behavioral changes can be experienced within a dependent relationship, the growth is not likely to last.

Even though being self-reliant is not necessarily a sign that one·is grown up, one cannot be grown up without being self-reliant. Having had the experience of being alone and somewhat self-sufficient makes it less threatening and painful to go through the emotional separation process. To complete that process, however, one must actually evolve from a dependent to an independent person within an ongoing relationship. The paradox of achieving separation within a union is difficult for many people, for they equate emotional separation with physical distancing. That this is not true can be seen by the distorted memories, fantasies, and nostalgia about our youth. How many times have you remembered a house or neighborhood a certain, idealized way only to be disappointed when visiting it? One patient spoke in such glowing terms of her early home that her therapist asked to see pictures. When the patient reluctantly brought in snapshots of a dilapidated, clapboard shack on a muddy street, they both laughed at her distortions. In the absence of reality confrontation, we tend to maintain our distorted view of the past. Because of this, dependent ties must be worked out concurrently with someone upon whom we rely.

Resolving the symbiotic tie with one's mothering one is not always possible. In addition to death, a debilitating illness, or remarriage, a parent may not be available because of emotional reasons. Parents who are overprotective or rigidly restrictive, for example, may be too anxious or threatened by separation to be responsive to such a development. Besides being worried that the youngster cannot adequately care for himself or herself, the nurturing parent may feel too empty and worthless without such a role. For a child to confront this parent with the need to individuate can be equivalent to parental murder. Under these conditions, transferring the struggle to a mate is not uncommon. However, leaving home for such a marriage is no more an indication of growing up than is getting a divorce. Although attempting to resolve one's dependency in a marriage without having completed this process at home is more difficult, it may be the only option available to many people.

THE NEW FRONTIER

Marriage provides another chance to grow up, but not everyone uses it that way. Many couples grow old together Hanging In with grandchildren, retirement villages, or travelling. There is a lot of togetherness but little intimacy. Attachments are ritualized, with few spontaneously joyful events between them. The most intimate moments are sharing losses and nostalgic recollections. There is a fear of letting go of fantasies about themselves and their marriage. The partners remain in a limbo together—not dead and not alive.

Other couples grow old together Giving Up. Illusions are gone. A hopeless resignation accompanies the loss of fantasies. They complain about each other and about life in general. They have very little future to look forward to and cannot enjoy each other in the present. Neither can they enjoy themselves separately, as they are stuck in their dependent position.

It is uniquely a phenomenon of our times that so many men and women still feel vital and alive through their fifties and well into their sixties. In an overview of marriage, raising children belongs to the first half. It is no longer a life's work or the principal reason that people couple and remain together. It is the second half of marriage—when husband and wife can be grown up, each complete unto himself or herself—that is, in large measure, a new frontier of unexplored marital territory. When marriage partners have the courage to accept reality and give up their illusions while struggling with each other to be more separate, they have a chance to bring to their relationship a new vitality. It is the liveliness of uncertainty and discovery: uncertainty about the outcome of confrontation and discovery of new dimensions in oneself and each other.

8
chapter

BECOMING:AN ONGOING PROCESS

In the course of Growing Up, each partner establishes independent areas of interest and activity. Some distinctive preoccupation, characteristic of one's outlook on life, emerges through work, a hobby, friends, or a particular TV program. This becomes one's "turf," that unmistakably separate interest that distinguishes one partner from the other. At times, such activities may be all-pervasive. Often, they are performed by rote. Occasionally, they clash with the needs of one's mate. But in this stage, they always are an integrated part of the connection called marriage. These personal trademarks are the raw material with which relationships are built. The energy invested in a marriage comes from this source. *A separate identity is necessary to sustain a mature relationship.*

An independent self-image is also needed to counteract the constant pull of the symbiosis. The urge to reestablish the dependent tie of long ago is ever present. It is like a habit. No matter how often you master it, there is always a tendency to revert. Under stress, or acute anxiety, the danger of returning to this earlier mode of relating is most pronounced. Individuals who have gone through the Growing Up phase of becoming a couple accept this continuous temptation as part of the reality of marriage—a force to be recognized, accepted, and dealt with effectively. They cope with this habitual pressure to regress by underscoring their separate identities.

EVOLVING A BALANCE

As a marriage progresses, each partner evolves a rhythmical balance between the need for independence and the need for unity. A personal ratio of detachment to connectedness is established by each spouse. Time, place, and emotional intensity are typically the chief variables that determine this ratio. Some people regulate their attachments principally through the use of time. Daylight hours are more likely to be spent away from one's mate, while evenings typically are spent together. When one spouse tells the other, "I could not stay away from you any longer," it may be a literal truth. Some individuals have a built-in clock that tells them when it is time to shift to another mode of being. They become moody and irritable if they overstay their state of relating. The tolerance for individuation may be greater, or less, than the capacity to maintain closeness. With experience, both partners learn to accept this interval as part of their dynamic interplay. The length of time one feels comfortable away from, or close to, a mate can change with experience and maturation.

Where one expresses oneself also determines the type of interpersonal involvement. Few mature couples are demonstrative in public. Yet they may feel free to be warm and affectionate to family and friends at parties and celebrations. Going away on vacation usually increases sexual ardor and physical closeness. Places of work, sports, recreational activities, and fraternal meeting rooms are generally attended without a mate. The couple's home and the homes of friends and family are places where partners share.

The emotional intensity associated with either separation or intimacy also determines in which of these states one is likely to engage. Most individuals have central nervous systems that go awry when they become overloaded. The amount of intensity they can tolerate will vary. However, everyone has limits. Some people panic if they are alone for two minutes. Others hyperventilate, get headaches, diarrhea, or some other ailment if they become too excited in a relationship. Each of us has a signal that tells us when our state of existence is shifting from comfortable to unpleasant. Generally, we do something to alter the situation when we receive such a message.

Time, place, and emotional comfort determine the balance in the detachment-to-connectedness ratio. One of the seeming paradoxes of life is that this ratio must be worked out by each person conjointly with his or her mate in order to be effective. How these specific separate identities merge into the coupling becomes the process of the marriage. The possible interactions for this merger are endless. Yet each couple evolves a characteristic blend peculiar to their union.

In growing-up couples such a process is always dynamic; that is, a tension exists between the needs for individuality and togetherness. There is a constant pull to get close and once united, to separate. Each state is temporary. Both partners of such a union know and accept the provisional nature of their condition. They are attuned to each other's needs and respect each other's space. At the same time, they attend to their own individuality, continuing to nurture their separate identities. Each partner adjusts his or her behavior so that the ebb and flow of the pair is synchronistic. Each mate accepts the responsibility for personal fulfillment while supporting the union. And they do this in tandem. The interaction of individuality and coupling becomes mutually supportive. Individual growth emerges from the close connection. Further close connections evolve from the two growing individuals. Thus, the parts and the whole of marriage are united in a self-sustaining system. It is a process where both the coupling and it's members are constantly evolving. Neither is ever complete. It is an ongoing process of becoming.

BECOMING: SOME EXAMPLES

The process of becoming—the interaction of individuality and coupling—can be seen in the following examples.

Marilyn was feeling particularly deprived and lonely. She had just completed three weeks of intensive work with terminally ill patients and their families. More than anything else she wanted Glenn to spontaneously recognize her condition, reach out, and take care of her. However, Glenn was inattentive, expressing instead his excitement with others. After her initial disappointment abated, Marilyn observed that Glenn reacted positively to people who extended themselves to him. She also noted that it had been a while since the two of them had gone out alone for dinner. Glenn seemed to go out of his way to include others. If she suggested they dine out, he either invited another couple or said he was too tired. If she complained about his lack of attention, he became annoyed. Overcoming her feelings of deprivation, Marilyn realized that *she* could take Glenn out! The more she thought about it, the greater her excitement. When she next saw him she said, "I would like you to be ready at seven o'clock tomorrow evening. I am taking you out for dinner." Glenn was intrigued and interested anew in his wife.

Marilyn and Glenn were returning from a ski trip. They had a particularly enjoyable weekend and were quite close and loving. Neither wished to end the experience. However, both had made appointments that could not be broken. They expressed their mutual desire to continue their loving relationship and decided it was not possible. Instead, they played a game. During the last few miles of their trip both pretended to be on a first date. They told each other how much they enjoyed being together and seductively suggested going away again soon. They took turns expressing what they would prefer to do on the next "date." They laughed at each other's outrageous fantasies for a reunion. When they arrived home, they kissed and hugged, saying goodbye at the door. Their emotional separation was completed as they crossed the threshold and were bombarded with demands and details requiring immediate attention.

DEVELOPING SENSITIVITY AND TIMING SKILLS

When shifting from individuality to coupling, or vice versa, we must take into consideration the needs and feelings of our mate. This requires a heightened sensitivity to our partner and adeptness in timing the move. The development of these skills is a complex process. The basis for such training is established in our early parent–child relationship. Here, we learn to live with a particular level of tension and anxiety, predicated on the manner in which our parents react to their environment—including us as children. As we try to alleviate the worries and concerns of our mothering one by behaving in ways we believe would please, we develop a sensitivity to the anxiety level of this parent. In time, we learn to predict when such a person will lose control, becoming upset, angry, and critical of us. We know when to intervene to keep such upsets to a minimum. We can placate, appease, stay out of the way, get sick, or bring the upset to a head by making ourselves the target of an outburst. The more skillful we become in influencing this parent, the greater our confidence. The more secure we are with our individuality, the greater our success in influencing this parent. The two conditions are mutually enhancing.

Interestingly, the movement between separation and attachment is accompanied by a range of excitement that tends to remain relatively fixed. As we achieve greater freedom—more flexibility and liberation from our dependencies—we find ourselves marching to an inner rhythm that stems from childhood. By attuning to our parents' level of tension and learning to alleviate this anxiety, we become accustomed to a range of excitement having as its polar points comfort and dread. As we mature, we tend to remain within the limits of this emotional lability. When we become too complacent, secure, or comfortable, we characteristically stir things up for ourselves. Sometimes we will even enter into relationships that, historically, have been disastrous. If the dread side of this range is pronounced, we are likely to cool our involvements. Something akin to an emotional homeostasis exists that keeps us from going too far in either direction. Since this range of emotionality evolved out of a relationship with our mothering one, it is most readily activated in the intimacy of marriage. It tends to surface most clearly in the individuality-to-connectedness ratio. Here, we can observe that overloading either state of being sets up a dynamic that leads to the other type of interaction.

Marilyn and Glenn were spending all their time together. They ate out every chance they could, attended concerts, and shared close moments with friends and family. Sex was frequent and exciting. They were enjoying each other so much that they cancelled earlier plans in order to spend Christmas together. They were so involved that they failed to make alternative arrangements. When vacation time arrived, Glenn felt tired and needed to rest. Marilyn, on the other hand, was gearing herself to skiing and love making. The first few days were spent relaxing at home. Glenn would have preferred to continue idling, but Marilyn was getting restless. She said, "I think I'll make plans to go to Vermont Wednesday." Glenn felt torn, ultimately compromising with, "If you wait until Friday, I'll go with you." When they departed on Friday, Glenn was markedly unenthusiastic. About a half hour into the trip he announced, "Look, I really don't want to go. I asked you to wait believing I would be up to going by now, but I'm still too tired. I would like to be with you, but I just can't get up the energy." Without hiding her disappointment, Marilyn reacted, "I waited for you because I thought you wanted to be with me. Let's go back. You stay home. I'll go by myself." They turned back, dropped off Glenn, and Marilyn proceeded to Vermont by herself.

Despite her enthusiasm, Marilyn found herself taking the easy runs on the slope, leaving the ski area early, and reading a great deal. At home, Glenn was attending to neglected chores, answering mail, and cleaning out his desk. Both were functioning in low key. Even their telephone conversations were perfunctory. After a week apart a strange thing occurred. Glenn dreamt that Marilyn died. Although not a believer in omens, he was very upset. His typical control melted as his feelings of dread grew. He had Marilyn paged on the slopes. He just had to know she was all right. Immediately, upon learning of Glenn's fear of losing her, Marilyn returned home. They embraced ardently and remained in physical contact all day. Glenn could not stop touching his wife. Their excitement having returned, they decided to spend the last weekend of their vacation at a hotel.

Remaining within the accustomed range of emotionality is most likely achieved through the flexibility of movement between individuality and connectedness, separation and attachment, autonomy and dependence, and self-fulfillment and pleasing one's spouse. The greater the confidence and skill to accomplish all these states, the greater the movement. The more options available in marital interaction, the more nimble and supple the shift from one condition to another. This interplay between polar states is a dance requiring the cooperation of both partners. Needing this cooperation, we are necessarily dependent on our spouse. Paradoxically, we achieve the greatest success in this dependency by sustaining our emotional separateness. To be emotionally separate, that is, having resolved our symbiotic dependency with our mate, does not mean that we are independent. On the contrary, it implies an acceptance of dependence and an ability to behave in ways that make it more likely such needs will be met. Rather than holding our mate accountable for personal fulfillment, we accept responsibility for gratifying our own wants. However, the emotional separateness necessary for maturation and Growing Up is constantly threatened by the Big Fear. This dread of losing a loving partner and being alone has its roots in the very nature of the life cycle.

DEALING WITH THE BIG FEAR

It is a natural progression of life that we move from total connectedness (in the womb) to total separation (death). In the beginning and in the end we are most completely blended into our environment. This occurs without effort or consciousness on our part. During the trip between these two states, we consciously try to replicate this subjective feeling of fulfillment. However, the moment we try—consciously attempt to bring about a union—we become aware of our separateness. Our yearning is for someone to reach out and connect to us. We wish them to spontaneously desire us and act on their impulses. This compels us to be available for invitations from others. When this occurs, the possibility of losing such attachments becomes conscious. This can be painful. The recognition of this dread of separation is employed in our most devastating form of punishment—solitary confinement. People who have been imprisoned in this way maintain their sense of self by remaining attached to someone or something in fantasy.

The need to interact to be more complete keeps us all necessarily dependent. It is a mark of this dependency that it promotes both our sense of self, through fulfillment, and threatens us, through separation anxiety. Needing our mate for gratification, we are compelled to behave conditionally. Generally, it is dangerous to antagonize this person but safe to please. Governing our conduct is the fear of separation from this partner. The paradox is that when we are less afraid of this loss, we can live with our dependency without being governed by it. It is a dynamic balance in the ongoing individuality-connectedness process that is continually maintained. We can be grown up and still feel threatened by loss and separation, even though we are not necessarily ruled by it.

Marilyn needed minor surgery. She had always handled illness in a manner that said, "Don't bother. I can take care of myself." This was her learned reaction to her mother's over-protectiveness. On this occasion she allowed herself to feel frightened. She shared her feelings with Glenn and told him she needed to know he would be with her. He reassured her and actually found pleasure in fussing over her. He felt effective and she felt cared for.

Marilyn could accept her dependence on Glenn precisely because she was confident of her independence. Earlier in marriage she could not allow herself to be aware of feeling frightened or of needing her mate. Even when her neediness overwhelmed her, she was not free to share it with her husband. There was too much danger of losing herself in a dependent relationship to risk such openness. It was because Marilyn was more separate and more accepting of responsibility for herself that she could tell Glenn she needed him. Previously, her dependence was expressed in seeking his approval and trying to placate him. She hid her vulnerability, expecting her husband to know how she felt and to behave accordingly. If he acted other than she expected, she concluded he no longer loved her and, therefore, had become insensitive to her. These early expectations and conclusions were part of Marilyn's defense structure, designed to protect her from getting hurt in an unrequited love. That she was, in this instance, able to drop these defenses is a sign of her growth.

To protect ourselves from the pain of rejection, criticism, loss of love, and loneliness, we develop defenses. As young children we are naturally helpless and dependent on our loving parents to remain positively connected to us. When they do not, we feel the sting and dread of separation. To salve such injury we may feign self-sufficiency, wallow in self-pity, fall asleep, run to seek substitute love, or find other forms of protection. Which methods of safety we evolve will largely depend on the circumstances surrounding our parent–child relationship. In time, these methods become organized into firm defenses that generally succeed in offering us screening from the pain of separation. When we reach adulthood, these defenses, which originally served to protect us, frequently become counter productive, preventing us from relating more completely to our mate. In addition, maintaining this guard can keep us from living more fully. In the Growing Up phase of marriage, renouncing the expectation of being taken care of by our mate is generally accompanied by a concomitant letting go of defenses. This does not mean we are defenseless. On the contrary, our more discriminate use of such self-protective devices fortifies our sense of security. We know better how to take care of ourselves *and* maintain a coupling connection at the same time.

Some defenses are so well established by adulthood that, for all practical puposes, they are beyond change. For example, there are people who can only feel autonomous by living alone. Once they cohabit with another, they reexperience a symbiotic dependence. The accompanying expectation of their partner to take care of them is so strong as to cause a regression in areas they have fully mastered many times over. These people have not experienced Giving Up. They generally have a history of terminating relationships without struggling beyond their dependent attachment.

WIDENING THE CIRCLE

The stages of coupling, as outlined in the preceding chapters, are not conceived as a linear process, proceeding from point A to B, then C, and so on. Rather, they are an organization of interactional phases which occur and reoccur in an ever widening spiral. There are many who live in a relatively narrow circle of involvement because they are too frightened or too resistive to follow their own process into the next natural stage. There are others who settle for a more placid life alone, rather than deal with the ongoing struggle inherent in trying to work out a relationship.

For those who make the commitment to remain connected *and* to live as fully as possible, the interactional stages of Becoming A Couple will be experienced again and again. The intensity of involvement and degree of awareness within each phase will increase each time around. A couple may travel the circle of The Loving Relationship, The Honeymoon Is Over, and Getting Even many times before moving to the next stage, Hanging In. What moves a couple into the progressive step is the commitment to find personal gratification while remaining in the union. This need for individual fulfillment makes it unlikely that partners are ready to move into the next stage of marital development at the same time. Such action usually is initiated by the spouse who is, at the time, most in pain, deprived, or stuck. The other spouse, despite confusion and upset over the shift in the status quo, will be carried along to the following stage by dint of holding on to the relationship. When partners follow their respective individualities, the relationship will naturally proceed to that stage of development that is best accommodated by the pair. The tension produced by this ebb and flow of connecting and individuating helps propel this process.

The rapidity with which a couple move through their development to the point of growing up will largely be determined by their respective security needs. Each participant in the dyad is undergoing change in the context of a constantly shifting environment. Sometimes the pace is dizzying. In the face of a chaotic, unpredictable world, the need for a secure reference point becomes pronounced. Using the marital relationship as a fixed resource to help deal with these external changes is very tempting. However, to do this tends to keep the marriage static. Trying to adjust to an environment that routinely punctures lifelong beliefs in government, honesty, frugal savings, sexual roles, and family allegiances can make anyone feel unsure. It is not uncommon to find modern men and women in the forefront of social innovations clinging to traditional marriages. While the need for firm identities, unchanged by circumstances, is understandable, it places limitations on the couple: The number of available options is cut down. Having less freedom to interact, the pair tend to remain in any given stage. The need for security thus slows the pace of the coupling process.

In addition to social pressures, personal insecurities may motivate partners to remain fixated in their marriages. One of the pair may become stuck in The Honeymoon Is Over phase because the power struggle of Getting Even is too threatening. On the surface the couple may appear devoted and loving. There is an exaggerated attempt to please that is overly sweet. However, the marriage remains frozen—seemingly secure but increasingly stale. If one mate should suddenly leap to Doing Your Own Thing (either out of interest or boredom), it will create havoc with the partner. The ensuing insecurity and fear of confrontation lead many people into psychotherapy. They are confounded by their shaky marriage in the face of their seeming loyalty. Another frequent point of marital fixation is the Hanging In stage because it is too frightening to risk the separation of Doing Your Own Thing. Many women employ their mothering role to resist individuating until it is time to separate from their children. At that point, they may find themselves living with a spouse who has outgrown them. The fear of separation from their mate may sufficiently motivate them to overcome their dread of risking an interaction with strangers. In either case, the personal insecurity leading to the snail's pace of marital progression may be the basis for suddenly jolting the marriage into rapid succession, leaving the couple breathless.

Couples who have achieved Growing Up feel more comfortable with themselves and use their marriage as an outlet for their individuality, rather than as a source of personal security.

This need for a stable attachment to deal with a changing and unpredictable world lessens as each partner becomes more connected to self and anchored in the present. People who are free to express themselves spontaneously worry less about their partner's reaction. They feel more secure and, consequently, more able to relate fully to their environment—including their partner. People who are most frightened of dying (separation) are most afraid to live. As more energy is invested in living in the present, less is available to worry about the future. Planning and responsibility occur in the context of self-enhancement, rather than as a security device. Feelings of insecurity, fear, and threat appear as in everyone else. However, individuals in Growing Up acknowledge and face such emotions while taking the responsibility to resolve them. One choice available to a member of such a coupling is to turn to the partner (as Marilyn did), express the painful feeling, and ask to be taken care of in specific ways.

The ongoing process of Becoming A Couple is further influenced by the respective personalities of the pair and their attendant characteristic styles of interaction. If an individual is stubborn, rigid, and determined to get his or her own way, he or she will generally linger in the Getting Even phase. Highly compliant and dependent individuals tend to cling to The Honeymoon Is Over phase. Rugged individualists favor Doing Your Own Thing. Hanging In is familiar territory for compulsives and those who are highly security conscious. Sometimes depressives and guilt ridden individuals find it difficult to get past Giving Up. Personality traits do have a bearing on the rate of couple development. They also tend to focus on specific phases more than others. When the characteristics of both partners are combined, the factors that determine where a couple are in their marriage and the rate of their evolvement become numerous.

It is also possible for couples to work toward Growing Up—as long as they remember that this stage, too, is only a plateau. It is not an ultimate state of marital being superior to all others. While it is the most difficult to attain in the developmental series outlined, it is not necessarily the best. Life circumstances, the needs of each partner, children, time, and innumerable other factors determine which stage is most appropriate for a particular couple at a given time. However, couples can take stock of themselves, each other, and their state of development and consciously move toward Growing Up. This conjoint effort, paralleled by successful individuating, can lead to an acceptance and appreciation of a working partnership with endless ongoing surprises and rewards. The key is ongoingness, flexibility, and a capacity to accept change.

RECOGNIZING AND ACCEPTING LIMITATIONS

Achieving Growing Up, partners recognize that they each are limited. Not all thoughts, feelings, behavior, or needs can be shared with each other. It is important to recognize what areas of functioning a partner cannot tolerate. This knowledge is necessary to intelligently decide which needs to share with a partner and which to gratify elsewhere. Although the most important and greatest number of personal attributes are typically shared with a marital partner, there are some aspects of being that are held back. A particular need may be withheld because a spouse is unavailable. He or she may be out of town, preoccupied, or sick. He or she may not have the skill, energy, or interest to share a specific need. His or her personal code may not permit some areas of expression.

A mature partner considers the personality and condition of a mate when deciding what to share in marriage. This discriminating choice is different from the holding back in The Honeymoon Is Over or Hanging In. There, the motivation for suppressing feelings is the fear of rejection and consequent loss of love. In Growing Up, those reactions directly meant for each other—anger, hurt, jealousy, appreciation, love—are fully expressed. In their interaction the couple are forthright, responsive, and respectful of each other's reaching out. One expression of this respect is the acceptance of a partner's limitations and the concomitant decision to omit sharing a troublesome issue. Although sharing generates caring, it is not a demand for a spouse to *do* something. Each needs the other's independence and right to maintain a private space. Neither invades the other without an invitation. Both accept the responsibility of deciding what, when, and how to connect as well as remain separate. Such responsibility sets Growing Up apart from all other stages of Becoming A Couple.

When a couple remain attached through the pain of individuating and the despair of Giving Up, one of the rewards of Growing Up is the confidence that your partner is also your best friend. Having shared in each other's growth, suffered through each other's failures and torments, a level of trust is built up that exists nowhere else. You know you belong because even your bodies have learned to fit together. Knowing this cushions that inevitable hurt and disappointment when you are desirous of your partner and he or she is not available. You tolerate this separation because you have the security of your unity. This confidence encourages the struggle for self-expression even when it means disconnecting from your spouse. Inherent in such strife lies the potential of unearthing new dimensions within yourself *and* a new kind of union with your mate. When you meet this challenge, you feel alive; uncomfortable at first, expansive later on. When such behavior is initiated by your partner, the sharpness of the pain of separation is softened by your knowledge that he or she means you no harm. You also take pride in your partner's growth and expansiveness. While you would like your partner to pursue his or her excitement with you, your curiosity in the outcome of his or her venture helps to bridge the gap. When you reunite, the sum of your respective individualities energizes the connection, encouraging new experiences and a creative interaction. You are in the process of becoming.

9
chapter

CONNECTING, SEPARATING, AND RECONNECTING

The ongoing process of becoming a couple is greatly influenced by the way we learn to connect, separate, and reconnect as children. Our earliest attachments occur outside our consciousness with our mothers' reaching out to us. Not until we experience separation and discomfort is there anything resembling a conscious effort on our part to reconnect with the lost parent. The timing and manner in which this connection-separation-reconnection sequence takes place largely determines whether we follow a smooth transition from dependency to autonomy or become fixated at specific stages along the way. The point where our normal developmental pattern is disrupted sets the phase of our later fixation. The younger we are when such events take place, the greater the impact on our development. The earlier the influence, the more likely all later stages will be affected. The more helpless our condition, the deeper the influence on our subsequent behavior.

The *intensity* of the interference in the normal connection-separation-reconnection pattern also influences our growth. The violent suicide of a parent is bound to leave a deeper scar on us than the short hospital stay of a nurturing mother. Being physically abused at one year of age is more likely to distort our growth than a neurotic experience at age seven. *What, when,* and *how severely* our developmental pattern is disrupted will determine our ultimate ability to evolve in the coupling process. The stage of marriage at which we are most likely to become fixated is related to that phase of growth affected by the trauma.

To illustrate this point, we, the authors, have selected two women whose growth was interrupted at approximately the same point in their development. In each case, inordinate dependency resulted from a very early trauma in the mother–daughter relationship. In one case the mother died; in the other, the parent was extremely overprotective. Both women developed strong fantasies. Throughout their maturation each had difficulty in the interpersonal area. Neither could connect deeply in reality, as their imagined pictures constantly disrupted the process. They resolved their sense of isolation by placating whomever they depended on. Both became fixated in The Honeymoon Is Over stage of marriage.

THE INFLUENCE OF
CHILDHOOD TRAUMA: SUSAN

It was nighttime and Susan was in bed with her husband. They had enjoyed an atypically pleasant evening going out to dinner and the theatre. Their affection carried over as they went to bed feeling warm toward each other. Susan's husband tentatively reached out and she responded to his touch. They moved along a familiar sexual path, both becoming more aroused until Susan's husband mounted her. She was readying herself for more intense action, leading to her usual diluted climax, when everything stopped. Her husband had ejaculated and was rolling off with a satisfied sigh. The combination of his satisfaction and her disappointment was too much! She began to yell and scream, working herself into hysteria, heaping insult after insult upon him until he left the bed and went to sleep on the couch in the den. A frightened and miserable Susan stayed awake most of the night. Although she had lived with deprivation and disappointment most of her life, never had she been so out of control. The next day, feeling guilty, terrified, and still angry with her husband, she made an appointment to see a psychotherapist.

At an early age, Susan lost her mother. This parent became ill with cancer when Susan was three and died when she was five. Susan was subsequently sent to live with an aunt until she was thirteen.

In young children the loss of a parent is usually accompanied by feelings of guilt. Even if a child does not feel directly responsible for the death, that child thinks he or she, somehow, could have prevented it. Susan's guilt feelings were helped along by her aunt. She claimed Susan was the cause of an infection which started her mother's illness.

While she was growing up, Susan attributed her unhappiness to being motherless. Anytime she was deprived or disappointed, she thought, "If only my mother were here, this wouldn't have happened." Her picture of her mother became idealized (a saintly woman who now lived in heaven with God). Her mother's love for her was also considered absolute. "If my mother were alive, she would do, or say, something that would make me feel better." Because of this, nothing in reality could ever match her internalized picture of love. As long as she maintained this fantasy, every attachment would be measured against it and found wanting. This left her feeling constantly deprived. She incorporated this deprivation into feeling deservedly punished (and therefore, less guilty) for causing her mother to die.

When Susan became a young woman, her thoughts of a loving mother were transferred to fantasies of a loving husband. After her wedding, the realities of marriage, love, mate, and sex proved horribly disappointing. As long as her deprivation could be attributed to her husband, she was able to remain somewhat in balance. When she felt frightened by her loss of control and unbearably guilty for driving her spouse out of bed, she could no longer function.

Early life traumas lead to fixations in our personality. The pain of these upsets are warded off through the establishment of characteristic defenses. These predictable behavioral patterns are designed to avoid experiencing the original blow to our egos. Although they protect us from expected hurt, they create a rigidity of behavior that keeps us mired in fixed arrangements. In marriage, we tend to become stuck in that stage of couple formation most closely resembling our defenses.

Susan's dependent personality was already well-established by the time of her mother's death. This trauma, however, led her to believe in her own basic malevolence and power to cause a loved one to leave. She defended against the pain of this self-image by a reaction formation, a denial of her natural aggressiveness. As a result, she became fixated in a placating role. Her typical marital behavior was to be available to please her husband. She remained fixated in The Honeymoon Is Over phase.

As long as Susan could sustain this role, she could function without too much anxiety. In time, however, her behavior intertwined with her fantasies. She developed strong expectations that her husband would be happy with her conduct and reward her by wanting to reciprocate. When neither expectation was met, her fundamental belief in the power of fantasy was threatened. The ensuing loss of control and attack on her husband frightened her more than the forfeiture of her fantasies. Her forbidden malevolence emerged to "blow the cover" of her placating ways. No longer could she sustain the picture of a compliant, passive, and helpless individual. Since her blow-up was spontaneous, authentic, and beyond her control, Susan could not deny her ability to be punitive and cause a loved one's departure. The threat of separation and loss of her husband reawakened the early trauma of her mother's death. This time, however, she could not return to her dependent orientation.

In individual psychotherapy, Susan dealt with the meaning and function of her fantasies. Once she learned to master her inordinate reliance on expectations, the therapeutic emphasis shifted to finding new ways for Susan to relate to her husband. Couple sessions were instituted, with assignments and tasks designed to help move the marriage beyond The Honeymoon Is Over stage. Success in these undertakings led to stability in the Hanging In phase of marriage. Here, Susan and her husband continue to explore creative forms of self-expression while sustaining the unity of their connection.

THE INFLUENCE OF
EARLY TRAINING: CAROLINE

In a viable marriage there is a constant interplay between the needs for security and growth. Remaining fixated in a particular phase of marital development may appear safe. When you behave spontaneously, however, this stage is no longer protection from either your fears or your partner. The fear of separation, especially for someone with a history of a lost parent, will always be an issue. As long as you feel positively connected to somebody, you can be hurt by the loss of this person. The choice is either to risk the struggle of a vulnerable relationship or to remain fixated. This can be seen in the case of Caroline where, unlike the case of Susan, there is a history of a relationship to a mother with an overwhelming presence.

Caroline needed to buy a mattress. She saw an advertisement in the newspaper, consulted her husband, and went to the department store to make the purchase. In the store she was confronted with an array of mattresses in addition to the one advertised. She became confused, could not make a decision, and left. On the way home she felt ridiculous. After tossing her thoughts back and forth, she turned the car around and returned to the store. Once again in the mattress department she became confused and anxious but placed an order for the advertised article. By the time she arrived home, she decided to cancel the order. Several days later, still without a mattress and unable to make a decision, she made an appointment with a psychologist.

When Caroline came into therapy, she had been married eight years and was the mother of two young children. Before marriage she had been a computer programmer in a small New England town. She had lived by herself, handled her needs adequately, and made hundreds of decisions daily without giving them a second thought. Why did this change so drastically after marriage and motherhood?

Caroline had been an only child with no siblings to dilute the intensity of her connection to her mother. Caroline's mother had strong ideas about how children should be raised and was free to devote her time and energy to molding her daughter. She studied her child constantly and was always ready with some advice for improvement. Caroline learned at an early age that "Children should respect their elders" and "Children should be seen and not heard." By the time she was three, she knew the rules of perfect child behavior by heart. When Caroline came to her mother with excitement about some new discovery, she generally received a lecture about being too rambunctious. She soon learned to keep her enthusiasms to herself and display only those aspects of her behavior deemed appropriate. Despite this deportment, Caroline's mother continued to be all-enveloping. Caroline remained dependent on this parent, to the exclusion of all others, until she went off to college. For the next nine years she functioned alone and well. Except for periodic visits home, she had no further contact with her mother. Her relationship with her husband was the first intense connection she made since leaving home.

It was not long before Caroline transferred her dependency onto her husband. They subscribed to the convention that he was to be the sole breadwinner while she attended to their home and family. She gave up working and all other outside interests. Her husband's job largely determined the location, style, and socio-economic level of their family life. This reinforced the subordinate position she assumed when she married. Having no other model for closeness, she never questioned her dependency; she automatically fell back into the same type of relationship she had with her mother. She was stuck in The Honeymoon Is Over phase of marriage, unable to get beyond trying to please her husband. Had Caroline not become a mother herself, or had she retained some outside identity, her lack of confidence would not have become so all-pervasive. However, after eight years of living such a limited existence, her psyche rebelled.

Caroline's primary character defense was repression. All those impulses, urges, and excitements labeled "bad", remained hidden from anyone she was close to. Instead, Caroline developed a rich inner life through fantasy. Here, she could imagine herself doing a thousand outrageous things. Everything forbidden in her actual relationships were given full expression in her thoughts. At the time of the mattress incident, Caroline could no longer keep them separate. She was no longer certain when an event occurred or whether she simply thought it. Her loss of confidence spilled over onto her shopping decision, paralyzing her.

Just prior to this incident, Caroline and her husband were unusually close. They were quite playful sexually, experimenting with a variety of techniques. Caroline, uncharacteristically, allowed her impulses free expression. She suddenly found herself the innovator and force behind the sexual activity. While her husband seemed to enjoy her role, she felt overwhelmed, confused, and frightened. She stopped immediately, stating she did not feel well. She thought she had put the incident out of mind, until the following week when she went shopping at the department store. The mattress triggered memories of lying in bed and having sex. The emotional experiences were similar and brought the return of feeling overwhelmed, confused, and frightened. At that point, Caroline was no longer clear which experience she was undergoing.

Through psychotherapy Caroline saw the function of her hidden life. She recognized the self-protective intent of these repressions. To avoid the threat of losing a loved one, she went underground. In its place, she offered a dutiful, placating, subordinate companion. She felt safe playing the dependent role. She knew she could get along quite well on her own and, therefore, believed that the regressive behavior in her close relationship would not affect her self-confidence. As with her mother, she rationalized her behavior with her husband. Her treatment provided a vehicle through which her individuality could emerge while remaining connected to the therapist. The next step was to assert that individuality with her husband, something for which her childhood training failed to prepare her. Thus began a long series of confrontations and power struggles (Getting Even) leading to Hanging In and Doing Your Own Thing.

Caroline's sense of self became more solid through the give and take of her new relationship. However, she will always have a problem with intimacy. When she becomes deeply involved with her husband, her boundaries become fuzzy and she begins to withdraw. Being aware of this difficulty enables her to share her discomfort and need to pull away with her husband. He, in turn, can feel supportive instead of confused and rejected. This permits them both to sustain a positive attachment much longer than was previously possible.

WAYS OF INTERACTING

There are many ways to relate. Any arrangement two people voluntarily agree upon can lead to a viable union. As long as both partners are essentially fulfilled and neither is exploiting the other, the interaction is healthy. But people do grow and change. What was an effective means of relating yesterday may be counter productive today. It all depends on the individuals and where they are in their development. When couples are committed to the marriage, the growth of one partner most often helps the other. With changes in both, the type of involvement will shift. Sometimes the differences are so subtle as to escape attention. Frequently, however, phases of interaction overlap so much that without a scorecard, it is difficult to know the status of your relationship.

Knowing how you and your spouse characteristically relate can help you make the most of your marriage. Also, recognizing the various kinds of interactions can provide more options for your coupling. To help you formulate where you are in your relationship, a summary of the most frequent types of interaction follows.

In The Loving Relationship, the principal orientation is love. A feeling of positive regard, heightened excitement and happiness, along with a desire to please your spouse, characterizes this stage. The wish for physical proximity, sexual relations, and the sharing of space is pronounced. Fulfilling your mate is tantamount to self-fulfillment. Your partner looks, feels, smells, tastes, and sounds beautiful to you. You are happiest when together. Apart, you are preoccupied with thoughts of your lover and direct most of your energies toward reuniting. You evoke recognition and special attention from friends and family. Your love radiates to those around you. Your partner connects to you with similar feelings. If not, you cannot remain very long in The Loving Relationship.

When you are trying chiefly to placate your partner, you are in The Honeymoon Is Over stage of marital development. Here, attempts at pleasing your mate through appeasement, catering, and self-denial are characteristic. During this phase you try to fulfill your spouse out of fear rather than love. Your mood is one of disappointment, confusion, and doubt. You may even feel desperate sometimes. There is a sense that something is wrong and needs correction, but just what and how is unclear. You concentrate on getting your mate to love you. You try harder. The relationship is no longer effortless. You make conscious efforts to change, hoping to please your partner. Eventually, you feel helpless and shift toward altering your spouse's behavior. You are quite sensitive, feel hurt, and may cry often during this period of your marriage. When both partners are in this stage together, it appears that each is giving to the other but nobody is getting.

You can tell that you are in Getting Even if a power struggle is typical of your interaction. During this stage, feelings of self-righteousness and deprivation predominate. These emotions are in the service of justifying the basically punitive behavior you inflict on your partner. Stubbornness, refusal to submit to your mate's wishes, and demanding to get your own way are most often observed. Blame, anger, and hurt are imposed on your partner during this phase of coupling. Frequently, money, sex, food, and time are points of contention. You focus on punishing your spouse until he or she submits to your view.

A combination of one partner in Getting Even and the other in The Honeymoon Is Over stage is also possible. While one spouse is critical and vindictive, the other is typically placating. This infuriates the first even more—often leading to physical force. Appeasement and self-criticism are poor rejoinders to someone who wants to feel effective in punishing his or her mate. This type of alliance is partially stable in sadomasochistic arrangements but is not recommended as an ongoing relationship for most couples.

When you find yourself taking your mate for granted, perfunctorily exchanging anecdotes while feeling strongly about other matters (your house or career, a child or friend) you are in Hanging In. When you sit in a restaurant watching others rather than your partner, talk "about" your activities, and hurry home to a TV program, you are in this phase of your marriage. You spend much of your free time away from home, generally expressing more excitement with others than with your spouse. During this period you displace your passion onto activities related to family. The intensity of your feelings is invested in people and interests that you and your mate perceive as part of your marriage. If you find that the only time you are sexually passionate is when you go on vacation, the odds are that you are in Hanging In.

When one spouse is at The Honeymoon Is Over phase while the other is in Hanging In, there is a discrepancy in the power expressed between them. The former appeases and caters to the latter, who is considered the productive member of the dyad. The Hanging In partner is overtly contributing to the welfare of the marriage, while the other plays a supportive role. This is the picture of the traditional pre-1950 marriage, with the wife in The Honeymoon Is Over role. It can be a stable arrangement, especially if there are children. Nowadays, however, both sexes are exposed to having their consciousness raised and neither is likely to settle for a subordinate role indefinitely.

The combination of a couple in Getting Even and Hanging In finds one punishing while the other displaces. This is a manifestly unhappy marriage, with fear the main ingredient in holding the pair together. Usually, it is the fear of separation that keeps them locked in. This leaves the Hanging In partner feeling contrite and defeated. No amount of success, retribution, or personal agony is acceptable to his or her spouse. The Getting Even partner feels cheated, measuring all behavior against a standard that only a fantasy can fulfill. Frequently, religious beliefs, children, and financial difficulties influence such a couple to remain married despite their misery.

When emotional gratification principally comes from your activities away from home, you are in Doing Your Own Thing. You may still be committed to your marriage and may have intensely loving moments with your partner, but your fulfillment takes place elsewhere. In this stage you look forward to going to school or work or seeing a friend, depending where your investments lie. You are proud of your accomplishments even though you may feel guilty relative to your spouse. Mostly, you enjoy a new-found confidence and are determined not to let your mate take it away. Your life seems lopsided and you wonder why you remain in a relatively sterile marriage.

Since you do not want to be permanently connected to anyone else, you stay. Besides, Doing Your Own Thing is fun and makes you happy—why spoil it? You are preoccupied with your personal involvements and no longer as concerned with your partner.

When one spouse is in Doing Your Own Thing and the other is at The Honeymoon Is Over phase, an idealization may be taking place. Such a pair look more like a parent–child dyad than husband and wife. Here, while The Honeymoon Is Over mate is catering and trying to please, the other spouse cannot wait to get back to his or her current interests. He or she may respond dutifully to the partner's solicitations but without any heart in it. Again, traditional marriages find the wife in the placating role. Such an arrangement has been used by many writers to depict a childlike wife who suddenly shifts to Getting Even, engaging in a series of torrid love affairs.

A Getting Even and Doing Your Own Thing union is very unstable and, unless the latter partner is unusually guilt ridden, will either shift to another type of interaction or dissolve. A confident mate, excited by outside activities, coming home to be criticized by his or her partner, is not likely to tolerate such treatment. Such an individual has a self-image that is too strong to accept punishment. Occasionally, a person who has progressed to Doing Your Own Thing will learn of a partner's involvement with another and regress to join the spouse in Getting Even. Although understandable, such an arrangement is terribly painful.

The combination of Hanging In and Doing Your Own Thing can be mutually supportive of each partner's personal growth. While one spouse is primarily attending to maintaining the family, the other is developing personal talents. Usually, such personal successes are brought back home to be reinvested in the marriage. When it occurs this way, the couple is often the envy of friends and neighbors. Sometimes, however, the Doing Your Own Thing partner remains involved with his or her personal interests to the detriment of the marriage. Also, the Hanging In mate may become jealous and decide spontaneously to shift to Doing Your Own Thing. As long as they maintain the primacy of their relationship, however, these partners are likely to enhance each other's interests.

Giving Up occurs when you finally realize that you cannot get what you always wanted from your mate. You also know that it is impossible to obtain it elsewhere. You renounce this wish. You feel sad and depressed but somehow stronger than ever. You begin to scrutinize your spouse, observing qualities you did not know existed. You feel more intimate while experiencing a distance in your relationship. Paradoxes abound. You feel confused and unsure of yourself as you affirm your conviction that your dreams will not come true. Tears, and an air of mourning, may pervade your existence. Many old values no longer hold. Finding replacements is not easy. You are more cautious; yet, more fully expressive. You are more completely in the present—even if it does not seem as beautiful as you had hoped.

The combination of a partner in The Honeymoon Is Over phase with one in Giving Up looks stable from the outside. Both are subdued, depressed, and apparently helpless. Each is disappointed—but for different reasons. The former because he or she still expects love to be forthcoming. The latter because the balloon has burst—he or she no longer has a fantasy to believe in. The two may be quite compatible in their suffering. However, the Giving Up partner is drawing strength from himself or herself while the mate looks to that partner for support. The more independent partner is likely to equalize the relationship by regressing to Do Your Own Thing, or else leaving the marriage.

A Getting Even partner with a Giving Up one form a relationship that is painful to sustain. While the former is out to punish, the latter has no illusions as to the mate's ability to satisfy him or her. The punishment has no leverage. Although success in inflicting pain may be achieved, no change is forthcoming from that partner. Frequently in this union, obesity, alcoholism, chronic depression, and physical illness are used to punish the Giving Up mate. Out of loyalty and devotion, the marriage is held together but the relationship's evolvement has all but stopped.

Hanging In and Giving Up pairs can complement each other. While one is displacing, the other is renouncing passion in the service of eliciting the partner's love. The emotional displacement of the former spouse serves to maintain a structure and stability to a relationship in which love and excitement are absent. The Hanging In partner is usually the more practical of the two, enjoying the relative calm of his or her spouse. As long as no major stress exists, both can be good humored and appreciative of each other's wit. Under pressure, however, they almost always polarize their positions. A horror to be near when there is family trouble, such a couple is a delight on vacation or when going out.

You can tell that you have reached Growing Up when your individuality and your marriage are expressed simultaneously. In this relationship you take full responsibility for gratifying yourself, including knowing when and how to ask your mate for help. You do not believe in magic and have no illusions that your partner will intuit your needs and spontaneously reach out to fulfill you. You are interested in your spouse and his or her personality and enjoy sharing new discoveries. Your sense of humor is at its best in this relationship as you devise creative ways to interact with your partner. Your marriage is full of surprises and your mate a constant source of innovative pleasure. And all this takes place while you are enjoying the pursuit of your separate interests.

A dyad consisting of a partner in The Honeymoon Is Over phase with one in Growing Up most likely is the result of regression on the part of the former. In traditional marriages, a wife sometimes expresses her liberated needs in rapid succession, developing abruptly from dependency to autonomy. The husband is often emotionally unprepared for the fast shift and reverts to The Honeymoon Is Over stage out of fear and hurt.

He tries placating his spouse, hoping to keep her from leaving him. She, in turn, perceives this maneuver and is determined to maintain her new-found freedom. Such a couple can sustain this arrangement for only a short time before changing to a different mode of interaction.

When Getting Even and Growing Up become the chief means of relating, sparks usually fly. This is a highly volatile combination, with punishment and intimacy alternately expressed. Such couples are generally very articulate and bright, verbally arguing with intense passion. The interchanges are highly sophisticated, and it is often difficult to detect which partner is expressing which orientation. However, the Getting Even spouse will usually succeed in hurting the other by using a self-revelation against him or her. All is fair in love and war!

Hanging In and Growing Up find displacement matched with direct expressiveness. This is a frustrating type of interaction, with the couple talking two languages. The Hanging In mate typically is self-righteous about all the benefits he or she bestows on the other through his or her responsible contributions to the family. The Growing Up member does not accept this argument. This mate does not believe that the other's sacrifices compel him or her to conform to that partner's view of proper behavior. He or she is an individual and refuses to be manipulated into adjusting to the partner's orientation. Both are, however, clearly investing their emotions in each other. Such a pair may continue relating thus for years before a change takes place.

When one spouse is in Doing Your Own Thing while the other is Growing Up, it is frequently difficult to tell them apart. They both appear autonomous and self-sufficient. Each has an active life that brings rewards. Both are usually independently successful, with their own set of admirers and friends. Such a couple seem well-integrated and secure. However, when they attend social functions together, they invariably become involved with others. They never look as if they are interested in each other. Indeed, during this phase of their marriage, they are not. The Doing Your Own Thing partner is busy substituting personal outlets for an emotional investment in the union. The other spouse is more philosophical, taking a leisurely, broad view of marriage and life in general.

You can always tell a couple who are in Giving Up and Growing Up by the morbidity of one while the other is good humored, encouraging, and supportive. They seem unbelievable. While the former appears pained and troubled, the latter is light hearted and gay. Free of expectations, such spouses appear oblivious of each other. Their behavior seems to have little to do with their partner's mood. Yet they are emotionally quite close and respectful of each other's condition. Such a couple typically have a long history of struggle and have learned to appreciate each other's strength. Alone, they can be quite romantic and sentimental. In the face of trouble they usually convey a faith that "This too will pass." They are a good bet to go on to Growing Up together.

OTHER INFLUENCES ON
MARITAL DEVELOPMENT

When identifying your relationship from among the types of interaction, observe that no sex distinction is in these roles. Either husband or wife may fit into any combination. These arrangements may result from an expansive drive for self-fulfillment or in reaction to hurt and disappointment. Also, the flavor and quality of any involvement will be influenced by the motivation of one or both partners. Generally, the movement from an early to a later stage is experienced as positive, optimistic, and hopeful. The regression from a more mature arrangement to an earlier one is usually reactive, frightening, and designed for self-protection. Try to remember that defensive behavior is geared toward avoiding pain and trouble. A couple who have arrived at Hanging In and then fall back to Getting Even will look quite different from a pair who have just advanced to Getting Even. This applies to individual progressions and regressions as well as to those carried out in unison by the couple.

Further, the style with which individuals and couples express themselves influences their marital development. One may be typically controlling and arrogant, regardless of which stage is being expressed. Have you ever seen a pompous and authoritarian placator? Or a sweet and tender punisher? They exist. Do not allow a person's style to interfere with your ability to define and identify which aspect of the relationship they are expressing.

Another issue to consider is the impact of perceiving your partner as receptive, rejecting, or indifferent to your behavior at any point on the continuum. Anticipating your mate's response will influence your actions. Regardless of your desire to move into Doing Your Own Thing, for example, expecting your partner's rage and fury can be enough to dissuade you from such a step.

Finally, bear in mind that love can be experienced by either or both spouses at any stage. In fact, as a partner progresses from one phase to another, there is often a resurgence of energy and emotion. This is especially true when a prolonged struggle at a particular stage is finally overcome and a breakthrough occurs. The power released by this pattern change frequently generates positive energy. This liberated pent-up love can be observed in any phase of becoming a couple—including Getting Even. In a later episode of *Scenes from a Marriage*, both partners dramatically release their suppressed anger after signing their divorce papers. The violent fight turns into a passionate embrace, with both partners risking their vulnerability precisely because they are about to separate. Watch for this release of energy at every juncture of your relationship.

SKILLS FOR A VIABLE UNION

Separating physically, as well as emotionally, is a necessary skill in coupling. The need to experience yourself independently is important in the individuation process. Moving from dependency to autonomy requires periodic activities where a testing of self-sufficiency can take place. Such information is vital to understanding where, how, and to what degree gratification is dependent on your mate. The accuracy of your estimate regarding what you contribute to and draw from your partner, is principally obtained in this fashion. Whatever objectivity you possess relative to your dependency-autonomy standing comes through this practice. Without it, getting beyond the symbiotic tie would be quite difficult. The trick is to accomplish this while remaining married.

Not infrequently, couples smother and stifle each other to the point of threatening the very existence of themselves and the marriage. This is not an overconnection due to excessive love or zeal; rather, it is mostly an attempt to prolong The Loving Relationship when this stage has passed. A yearning to recapture the authenticity of loving feelings, fear of losing a positive connection, and habit combine to make this kind of holding on an unhealthy transaction in marriage. Such behavior often continues because neither partner has developed the skill to solve this problem without threatening a break in the union. Recognizing the reality of this threat, husbands and wives alike strive to revitalize their coupling by taking time away from each other, engaging in specific interests alone, and even arranging for separate living quarters for varying periods. Once identifying the problem, it is important to share a no-fault view of the issue, and its possible solution, with your partner. Keeping your mate informed of your progress in overcoming the strangling effects of dependency also helps to make this a concern of the marriage, rather than a bad, or neurotic, trait that must be exorcised.

The connecting-separating-reconnecting skills necessary for a viable union can be seen in the progress made by the couples cited in previous chapters. For example, Julie and Tom (Chapter 2) went from trying to please each other to an intense power struggle. This lasted, off and on, for two years, finally culminating in physical violence. When the dust settled, their relationship shifted. Each accepted responsibility for the violence and recognized that their marriage could not tolerate a repetition of such anger. They were impressed with the intensity of their passion, as well as with their commitment to remain together. They stabilized their relationship by moving into the Hanging In stage via purchasing and remodeling a dream house. They were prepared to let go of *some* of their ideas of marital bliss.

For three years Pam (Chapter 3) was in individual and group therapy, where she struggled to define and express herself. Sharing her fear of closeness with Brian was followed by the release of her loving feelings for him. She became sexually responsive and initiating. This helped Brian feel greater security in the marriage. During this period, as part of her attempt to individuate and define herself, Pam got into Doing Your Own Thing by starting her own business. Brian's negative reaction might have previously drawn her back into the power struggle, but Pam's new-found awareness of her needs and goals prevented this from happening. She was determined to pursue her own interests while remaining connected to Brian. So far, she is succeeding.

After her daughter entered school, Wendy (Chapter 4) began seriously to move toward Doing Your Own Thing by getting a job in an office far removed from her husband. David reacted to this loss of power and control by threatening to separate. In a surge of anger, representing an accumulation of too many years of feeling frightened and restraining herself, Wendy countered by consulting an attorney for a divorce. David was devastated, offering all kinds of compromises and promises. Wendy, however, was adamant. Having made the break, she plunged into the separation which, initially, had so terrified her.

On the other hand, Lucille and John (Chapter 5) are having a ball. Their marriage has become more stable and egalitarian. They swing between Hanging In and Doing Your Own Thing. They are predominantly loving, rather than antagonistic. John has developed more self-confidence and learned to live with less pressure. He has become a really fun person.

Sheila and Bob (Chapter 6) alternate between Hanging In, Doing Your Own Thing, and Giving Up. Their emotional tone is for the most part still depressive. However, they did get a lift from reading the account of their struggles in these pages. They felt proud of their relationship and each other and optimistic about getting together in a more fulfilling way in the future.

Growing Up continues to offer Marilyn and Glenn (Chapter 7) a vehicle through which they can express their love for each other while engaged in separate activities. They are constantly surprised at their relief when one of their children terminates a visit, leaving them to enjoy each other. Family and marital duties are practically nonexistent. Instead, Glenn spends a great deal of time fishing and relating to his friends. Marilyn is busy rediscovering her mother and organizing a new department of social work in her office. In between, they manage to take trips together and are planning an elaborate addition to their beach house.

FOLLOWING YOUR OWN TRUTH

Learning the skills to connect, separate, and reconnect while maintaining integrity takes time, courage, and the strength to face the consequences of spontaneity. Relating intimately requires following your own truth and the wisdom of your coupling. It means overcoming the temptation to measure your behavior according to the fantasies and idealizations of a happy marriage presented in the movies, on TV, and in most advertisements. Try to remember that these images of marital bliss are designed by the hucksters to sell you their products—not to help your relationship. Besides authenticity, you need only count on your commitment to maintain your primary connection with your mate and your vow to face change with an open mind.

People resist change, tending to cling to what is familiar out of their need for security. Perceiving marriage as an evolving system with identifiable stages may help you flow with the coupling process, rather than fight it. Who is right or wrong (a familiar quarrel at any marital stage) becomes a moot question. Instead, dealing with your partner's need to connect and separate, with the resultant feelings of love, hurt, anger, or disappointment, and attempting to work out such a move are a much wiser investment of your energies. The most favorable background for interactions is one in which both partners accept the inevitability of change.

While we, the authors, recognize the potential benefits of working out a mutually enriching relationship, in the long run most people marry and divorce at the dictate of their feelings. For those pairs who do agree on the desirability of working past the difficulties in their marriage, the developmental view presented here should provide a perspective that promotes a positive outcome. Knowing that symbiotic dependency is a natural and necessary tie when two people fall in love may help each partner enjoy that dependency. Accepting the subsequent necessity for individuation may soften the hurt and anger accompanying separation. Finally, understanding the inevitability of giving up expectations and illusions may help one or both partners accept that stage of the process. Becoming a couple is not easy—but it is the best thing we have going.

GLOSSARY

Association Is the togetherness of two or more people that is time, space, or goal limited.

Attachment is togetherness with the individuality of at least one partner suppressed.

Connection is the dynamic interplay between individuality and attachment where the present needs of both partners are being met.

Couple is two people who are committed to each other in a primary relationship. Over a period of time they connect, separate, and attach while maintaining the primacy of their arrangement. Despite prolonged absences, sexual and emotional affairs, open hostility and rejection, they remain a couple as long as they are primarily committed to the relationship. Occasionally, even after divorce two people can remain a couple.

Fixation is a state of being where one's feelings and perceptions are relatively frozen at an early stage of personality growth. All subsequent experiences are influenced by this psychological retardation. Fixations associated with one's parents repeat themselves in couple formation and development.

Formation is the manner in which a particular behavior or behavioral pattern is formed. In *reaction formation* individual behavior is formed in reaction to a particular feeling or experience. *Couple formation* describes the progressive interactional behavioral pattern of the two partners.

Fulfillment Dependency is the recognition of the need for another and obtaining gratification of this need.

Individuation is becoming a separate and distinct being with awareness of personal needs and acceptance of personal responsibility for their fulfillment.

Loss is permanent separation in a coupling.

Marriage   is a commitment to a primary relationship on the part of each partner.

Relationship   is an ongoing association between two or more people that includes connection, separation, and attachment.

Separation   is the dynamic interplay between individuality and attachment where at least one partner recognizes that a present need is not being met.

Symbiosis   is the mutually interdependent relationship of two people where the dependent needs of one fulfills the other.

INDEX

Index